GOD'S CREATIVITY AND HUMAN ACTION

PREVIOUSLY PUBLISHED RECORDS OF
BUILDING BRIDGES SEMINARS

The Road Ahead: A Christian–Muslim Dialogue, Michael Ipgrave, editor
(London: Church House, 2002)

*Scriptures in Dialogue: Christians and Muslims Studying the Bible and the
Qur'ān Together*, Michael Ipgrave, editor (London: Church House, 2004)

Bearing the Word: Prophecy in Biblical and Qur'ānic Perspective, Michael
Ipgrave, editor (London: Church House, 2005)

Building a Better Bridge: Muslims, Christians, and the Common Good, Michael
Ipgrave, editor (Washington, DC: Georgetown University Press, 2008)

Justice and Rights: Christian and Muslim Perspectives, Michael Ipgrave, editor
(Washington, DC: Georgetown University Press, 2009)

Humanity: Texts and Contexts: Christian and Muslim Perspectives, Michael
Ipgrave and David Marshall, editors (Washington, DC: Georgetown
University Press, 2011)

*Communicating the Word: Revelation, Translation, and Interpretation in
Christianity and Islam*, David Marshall, editor (Washington, DC:
Georgetown University Press, 2011)

Science and Religion: Christian and Muslim Perspectives, David Marshall,
editor (Washington, DC: Georgetown University Press, 2012)

Tradition and Modernity: Christian and Muslim Perspectives, David Marshall,
editor (Washington, DC: Georgetown University Press, 2012)

Prayer: Christian and Muslim Perspectives, David Marshall and Lucinda
Mosher, editors (Washington, DC: Georgetown University Press, 2013)

Death, Resurrection, and Human Destiny: Christian and Muslim Perspectives,
David Marshall and Lucinda Mosher, editors (Washington, DC: Georgetown
University Press, 2014)

The Community of Believers: Christian and Muslim Perspectives, Lucinda
Mosher and David Marshall, editors (Washington, DC: Georgetown
University Press, 2015)

Sin, Forgiveness, and Human Destiny: Christian and Muslim Perspectives,
Lucinda Mosher and David Marshall, editors (Washington, DC: Georgetown
University Press, 2016)

GOD'S CREATIVITY AND HUMAN ACTION

Christian and Muslim Perspectives

A Record of the Fourteenth Building Bridges Seminar

Hosted by Georgetown University
School of Foreign Service in Qatar
May 3–6, 2015

LUCINDA MOSHER and
DAVID MARSHALL, *Editors*

Georgetown University Press / Washington, DC

The publisher is not responsible for third-party websites or their content. URL links were active at time of publication.

Library of Congress Cataloging-in-Publication Data
Names: Building Bridges Seminar (14th : 2015 : Doha, Qatar) | Mosher, Lucinda, editor. | Marshall, David, 1963- editor.
Title: God's creativity and human action : Christian and Muslim perspectives : a record of the fourteenth Building Bridges Seminar ; hosted by Georgetown University School of Foreign Service in Qatar, May 3/6, 2015 / Lucinda Mosher and David Marshall, editors.
Description: Washington, DC : Georgetown University Press, 2017. | Includes bibliographical references and index.
Identifiers: LCCN 2016052170 (print) | LCCN 2017006454 (ebook) | ISBN 9781626164857 (pb : alk. paper) | ISBN 9781626164840 (hc : alk. paper) | ISBN 9781626164864 (eb)
Subjects: LCSH: Quran—Theology—Congresses. | Bible—Theology—Congresses. | Creation (Islam)—Congresses. | Creation—Biblical teaching—Congresses.
Classification: LCC BP166.23 .B85 2015 (print) | LCC BP166.23 (ebook) | DDC 297.2/83--dc23
LC record available at https://lccn.loc.gov/2016052170

♾ This book is printed on acid-free paper meeting the requirements of the American National Standard for Permanence in Paper for Printed Library Materials.

18 17   9 8 7 6 5 4 3 2   First printing

Printed in the United States of America

Cover design by Debra Naylor.
Cover image by Shutterstock.com.

CONTENTS

PARTICIPANTS IN BUILDING BRIDGES SEMINAR 2015

Professor Asma Afsaruddin, Indiana University, Bloomington, Indiana

Dr. Shabbir Akhtar, University of Oxford, United Kingdom

Dr. Muhammad Modassir Ali, QFIS at Hamad bin Khalifa University, Qatar

Professor Ahmet Alibašić, University of Sarajevo, Bosnia & Herzegovina

Professor Najib Awad, Hartford Seminary, Hartford, Connecticut

Professor Richard Bauckham, University of St. Andrews, Ridley Hall, Cambridge, United Kingdom

Professor Jonathan A. C. Brown, Georgetown University, Washington, DC

Professor Maria Massi Dakake, George Mason University, Fairfax, Virginia

President John J. DeGioia, Georgetown University, Washington, DC

Reverend Dr. Susan Eastman, Duke University Divinity School, Durham, North Carolina

Dr. Brandon Gallaher, University of Exeter, United Kingdom

The Reverend Lucy Gardner, St Stephen's House, University of Oxford, United Kingdom

Professor Sidney Griffith, Catholic University of America, Washington, DC

Professor Feras Hamza, University of Wollongong in Dubai

Professor Tuba Işık, University of Paderborn, Germany

Professor Paul Joyce, King's College London, United Kingdom

Professor Mohsen Kadivar, Duke University, Durham, North Carolina

Professor Veli-Matti Kärkkäinen, Fuller Theological Seminary, Pasadena, California

Professor Katsuhiro Kohara, Doshisha University, Japan

The Right Reverend Michael Lewis, Anglican Diocese of Cyprus and the Gulf, Cyprus

Professor Daniel Madigan SJ, Georgetown University, Washington, DC

The Reverend Dr. David Marshall, Berkley Center for the Study of Religion, Peace and World Affairs, Georgetown University, Washington, DC

Dr. Jane McAuliffe, Distinguished Visiting Scholar, Library of Congress, Washington, DC

The Reverend Dr. Thomas Michel, SJ, Georgetown University School of Foreign Service in Qatar

Shaykh Ibrahim Mogra, Muslim Council of Britain

Professor Dheen Mohamed, QFIS at Hamad bin Khalifa University, Qatar

Dr. Lucinda Mosher, Hartford Seminary, Hartford, Connecticut

Professor Sajjad H. Rizvi, University of Exeter, United Kingdom

Professor Abdullah Saeed, University of Melbourne, Australia

Professor Feryal Salem, Hartford Seminary, Hartford, Connecticut

Dr. Hansjörg Schmid, University of Fribourg, Switzerland

Professor Christoph Schwöbel, University of Tübingen, Germany

Professor Ayman Shabana, Georgetown University School of Foreign Service in Qatar

Professor Philip Sheldrake, Westcott House, University of Cambridge, United Kingdom

Professor Sohaira Siddiqui, Georgetown University School of Foreign Service in Qatar

Professor Umeyye Isra Yazicioglu, St. Joseph's University, Philadelphia, Pennsylvania

INTRODUCTION

THIS BOOK PRESENTS the proceedings of the fourteenth annual Building Bridges Seminar, convened at the Georgetown University School of Foreign Service in Doha, Qatar, May 3–6, 2015, with university president John J. DeGioia present as host and participant. Launched in 2002 as an initiative of the Archbishop of Canterbury—and with the stewardship of Georgetown University since 2013, this gathering of scholar-practitioners of Islam and Christianity convenes annually, alternating between Muslim-majority and Christian-majority contexts, for deep study of selected texts pertaining to a carefully chosen theme. The circle of participants is always diverse ethnically and geographically, and balanced evenly in the number of Muslims and Christians—with a substantial number of women included in each group, and with a few emerging scholars joining the seasoned experts. Among the Christian scholars—who have always been for the most part Anglican or Roman Catholic—are usually included Orthodox and Protestant scholars as well, and this was the case in 2015. Similarly, while the Muslim participants are predominantly Sunnī, Shi'ite scholars have always been included. Since 2013 Daniel Madigan SJ, Jeanette W. and Otto J. Ruesch Family Associate Professor in Georgetown's Department of Theology, has served as chair of the proceedings.

Qatar is a familiar venue for the seminar. We were hosted in Doha in 2003 by the emir of Qatar, and on the Georgetown campus in 2011 and again in 2013. As has often been the case, the seminar commenced with a pair of evening lectures at an event open to the public. The three workdays of the seminar—all in closed session—followed a fixed pattern: a morning lecture on the topic for the day, in preparation for two hour-long small-group text-study sessions; an after-lunch lecture, likewise followed by two hour-long small-group text-study sessions; and late-afternoon summary discussion in plenary. This volume provides the reader with edited versions of the eight lectures, arranged here in pairs.

In part 1, readers will find the 2015 seminar's public lectures: "Human Action within Divine Creation: A Muslim Perspective" by Mohsen Kadivar (Duke University) and "On the Possibility of Holy Living: A Christian Perspective" by Lucy Gardner (University of Oxford). These are overviews, each laying out the complexity of the seminar's theme and some directions for deeper study. Kadivar concentrates on the exoteric approach to the matter, which itself ranges from ultraliteralist to maximal rationalist, as it plays out in Islamic theological and philosophical writings. He introduces such topics as God's unity, immanence, and transcendence; humanity's task, thus the nature of vicegerency; and the relation of God's attributes to matters of predestination and freedom of choice regarding human action within God's sovereignty. Gardner offers what she calls "a brief personal, theological guide to negotiating the thematic landscape" regarding the nature of human existence and human freedom. Thus, she explains the Christian doctrine of Creation as a matter of learning to see and understand the whole universe, including the ongoing characteristics of human beings as creatures in the light of its relationship with God—which in turn leads to consideration of the relation of the doctrine of Creation to the doctrines of Trinity and Incarnation, and the conviction that, according to scripture, humanity is created in God's image. She then explores notions of human intimacy with God, human virtue and creativity, and the possibility of holy living.

The structure of parts 2, 3, and 4 are identical. Each features a pair of essays introducing a seminar subtheme from a Christian perspective, on the one hand, and a Muslim perspective, on the other. These essays—in most cases a transcript of a lecture heard in closed morning plenary by the seminar participants—lay out important aspects of the given topic, focusing on some of the scriptural material chosen for that day's study sessions. Thus, in part 2, "God's Creation and Its Goal," Richard Bauckham (University of St. Andrews) offers a Christian theological account of the difference between creation and Creator, and between God's creative activity "at the beginning" and subsequent divine activity in the world. He offers insights into the notion of creation ex nihilo and the relation between divine creativity and divine love. Quite interesting is his account of the various Hebrew terms associated with God's creative acts. In providing a Muslim perspective, Sohaira Zahid Siddiqui (Georgetown University) expounds on God's attributes as they relate to divine creation, humanity's obligations to God, the various modes of divine creation, and the continuousness of divine creation.

In part 3, "The Dignity and Task of Humankind within God's Creation," Brandon Gallaher (University of Exeter), in his essay "Creativity, Covenant, and Christ," argues that it is only by coming to see creation as a theophany—as a manifestation of God's glory—and our lives as pure offerings of gratitude to God that human beings can attune themselves with the creative Word of God. Thus, he begins with the notion of creation as a divine gift and the relationship of covenant to creation, in order to delve into the Christian understanding of the uniqueness of humanity as created in the image of God with a "mediatorial vocation." The vehicle of this vocation is "obedient praise or glorification of God with the offering up of the self as pure and willing sacrifice through a holy life." This includes stewardship of creation.

In her essay, "To Be *Khalīfa*: The Human Vocation in Relation to Nature and Community," Maria Massi Dakake (George Mason University) explores the Islamic tradition that vicegerency—understood both individually and communally—is a noble role distinguishing humankind from the rest of creation. At the same time, it is a role beset by a unique set of moral challenges and fraught with moral peril. Thus, she discusses the Qur'ān's account of the establishment of Adam (and, by extension, of all humanity) as *khalīfat Allāh fi'l-arḍ*. Dakake examines various Qur'ānic passages that speak to the question of human relationship to, and moral responsibility for, other sorts of creatures and the Qur'ānic notion that human beings have a responsibility to form and maintain moral communities among themselves.

Writing on the theme of part 4, "Human Action within the Sovereignty of God," Veli-Matti Kärkkäinen (Fuller Theological Seminary) highlights the complex dynamic between divine sovereignty and human initiative evident in Christian scripture and explains ways in which the Christian theological tradition has sought to make sense of it. In the process, he offers a Christian perspective on such interrelated themes as the implications of the conviction that humans act within a creation that is to a large extent given; that humans act in relationship to the sovereign Creator who is even now at work; the question of whether human freedom is real or illusory—thus the degree to which our actions are in fact "ours"; and how petitionary prayer fits into a Christian understanding of the interplay between divine and human action. In his companion essay, Feras Q. Hamza (University of Wollongong in Dubai) helps us understand the sources of the Arabic vocabulary in Islamic discourse about the theological conundrum of human free will versus divine predetermination. As he lays out their complexities, he argues that, while early Muslim theological debates over these matters were anchored in "intra-Muslim religious polemics over urgent political questions," they also had deeply devotional aspects, conducted as they were by Muslims who were themselves "paragons of piety."

In parts 2, 3, and 4, the essay pair is followed by the compilation of Bible and Qur'ān passages that the seminar participants studied in their small groups. With the essays and the scripture anthology, the reader now has, in effect, a handbook for conducting a dialogical study on the overarching theme of human action within divine creation, or on any of the three subthemes.

By way of conclusion, part 5 comprises "Discussion in Doha," an essay in which Lucinda Mosher digests the small-group conversations that are the heart of the project.

Readers of *God's Creativity and Human Action* may desire suggestions for further engagement with the themes on which this volume focuses. For Christian perspectives, see Alexander S. Jensen, *Divine Providence and Human Agency: Trinity, Creation and Freedom* (Ashgate, 2014); John Cowburn SJ, *Free Will, Predestination and Determinism* (Marquette University Press, 2007); and Michael F. McLain and W. Mark Richardson, eds., *Human and Divine Agency: Anglican, Catholic, and Lutheran Perspectives* (University Press of America, 1999). For Islamic points of view, see Maria De Cillis, *Free Will and Predestination in Islamic Thought: Theoretical Compromises in the Works of Avicenna, al-Ghazali and Ibn 'Arabi* (Routledge, 2013); Sabine Schmidtke, ed., *The Oxford Handbook of Islamic Theology* (Oxford University Press, 2016); and Tim Winter, ed., *The Cambridge Companion to Classical Islamic Theology* (Cambridge University Press, 2008).

Throughout this volume, when not indicated otherwise in the text or endnotes, excerpts from the Qur'ān are according to M. A. S. Abdel Haleem, *The Quran: A New Translation* (Oxford: Oxford University Press, 2004) or are the essay author's own translation. Unless otherwise indicated in the text or notes, Bible passages are according to the New Revised Standard Version of the Bible, copyright © 1989 by the Division of Christian Education of the National Council of Churches of Christ in the USA. Used by permission. All rights reserved. An exception is the essay by Lucy Gardner, in which all Bible quotations are according to the Revised Standard Version of the Bible, copyright © 1946, 1952, and 1971 National Council of the Churches of Christ in the United States of America. Used by permission. All rights reserved worldwide.

Deep appreciation is extended to Georgetown University president John J. DeGioia for his ongoing support of the Building Bridges Seminar. The staff of Georgetown University School of Foreign Service–Qatar were gracious hosts. As for previous seminars, David Marshall (the project's academic director) and Daniel Madigan (its convener) took leadership in setting the theme, organizing the circle of scholars, and choosing the texts to be studied. Many people played a role in the success of the 2015 gathering, particularly Lucinda Mosher, who serves the project as assistant academic director, and Samuel Wagner, coordinator for Catholic and Jesuit Initiatives in the Office of the President, who provided logistical support.

Georgetown University's Berkley Center—particularly, its director, Thomas Banchoff—provides a base of operations and online presence for the seminar and has made the publication of this book possible. Finally, gratitude is extended to Richard Brown and the staff of Georgetown University Press.

PART I

Overviews

Human Action within Divine Creation

A Muslim Perspective

MOHSEN KADIVAR

HUMAN ACTION WITHIN divine creation has been the subject of long and controversial discussions among Muslims since the eighth century, first as the subject of study and debate in commentaries on the Qur'ān and Ḥadīth and then continuing as one of the first problems of Islamic theology. The Muslim philosophers and mystics engaged deeply in the subject and enriched its literature from their specific perspectives.

We may classify the Muslim perspectives on this important subject under esoteric and exoteric approaches. The perspective of all mystics such as Ibn al-'Arabī and some philosophers such as Shahab al-Din Suhrawardī and Mulla Sadrā, in some of their works (not all of them), is classified as "esoteric." I will not mention this approach in this essay.

I limit myself to the "exoteric approach," which comprises a wide spectrum from the ultraliteral interpretation of Zahiris to the maximal rationalism of Muslim philosophers such as Avicenna and Averroes. This spectrum can be seen as having two subcategories: thought that is best understood as "Islamic theology," which is relatively more textual and less rational, and thought that is more properly understood as "Muslim philosophy," which is more rational and less textual.

The theological perspective includes eight schools of thought: Ash'arī, Māturidī, Ḥanbalī, and the banned Mu'tazilī in Sunnī Islam; Ja'farī, Zaydī, and Ismā'ilī in Shi'ite Islam; and finally 'Ibāḍī. The philosophical perspective includes four schools of thought: peripatetic, illuminative, transcendent, and independent philosophers such as Muḥammad ibn Zakariyyā al-Rāzī, al-Bīrūnī, Fakhr ad-Dīn ar-Rāzī, and Abu'l-Barakāt al-Baghdādī.

Providing a general overview of twelve schools of thought on one of the most controversial problems in the history of Islam is not easy. I will focus on the key similarities and differences between these two main perspectives without going into the details and the apologetic debates. I will offer major verses of the Qur'ān and a few ḥadīths for each perspective as the main evidence—as well as a few theological or philosophical arguments. My goal is to demonstrate how Muslims, especially at the present time, understand human action within divine creation.

Introductory Remarks on the Unity of God

There is consensus among Muslims—regardless of their different schools, sects, and perspectives—that the cornerstone and inseparable master principle of Islamic thought is the unity of God (tawḥīd). This master principle has at least four levels: unity of God's essence (al-tawḥīd al-dhāti), unity of His attributes (al-tawḥīd al-ṣifāti), unity of His actions (al-tawḥīd al-ʾafʿālī), and unity of worship (al-tawḥīd ʿibāḍī). Although there are different understandings in the second and third, there is unanimity in the general understanding of the first and the fourth. Human action within divine creation is a factor at two levels of controversy regarding the unity of God: on "unity of His actions" (for the most part), and on "unity of His attributes" (to a lesser degree). To have a better understanding of the challenge, we must elaborate on the first level of tawḥīd—that is, unity of God's essence and its effect to other levels of this master principle of Islam.[1]

Deep study of the visible world (ʿālam al-shahāda), or natural world, teaches us that the actions and reactions of all particular beings—regardless of whether they be earthly or heavenly beings—are in intrarelation to each other, and there is no being out of this framework. Every action or reaction relates to the whole universe. From this fact we can infer a kind of unity, a large system designed and run by one operator. This is the first principle.

This natural, visible world could not be spontaneous. It is contingent and an effect of God—directly, as some "occasionalist theologians" in the Ashʿarī school (such as al-Ghazālī) believed, or indirectly, with the mediation of a chain of vertical, intellectual, immaterial causes (or angels), as all the Muslim philosophers and some theologians (such as Nasīr al-Dīn al-Tūsī) believed. According to both approaches, the ultimate originator of the world in all of its parts and aspects is no one except God. This is the second principle.

According to the principle of cause and effect, the cause of the cause of a thing is finally the cause of that thing, and the effect of the effect of a thing is finally the effect of that thing. When all of the causes lead to the Ultimate Cause—that is, God—it means that all beings, regardless of what they are, are His effects. There is neither independent existence nor any necessary being in itself except God. There is no originator of existence except God. This principle is clear in occasionalism too. It is the meaning of unity of God-as-Sustainer (al-tawḥīd fīʾl-Rububiyya). No god but God (Lā ilāha illā Allāh).

In the other words, God is the complete cause (adaquata causa; al-ʿilla al-tāmmah) for all beings as well as their agent cause (efficient cause; al-ʿillah al-fāʿiliyyah). He is independent in His origination absolutely as well as self-subsistent in His existence and causality. He is the real one who effects. There is no one who effects in existence except God. He is the agent of all things, and all the causes are as His agents—subjects and contingent to Him. It is the common ground of Islamic thought, and all Muslims are unanimous without any differences in the master principle of unity of God.

God's Creation and His Goal

What is God's goal in creation? Why is there anything at all? Why isn't there "nothing"? Why does God create in general? These are the questions of teleology and philosophy. I will discuss three issues in this section: God's goal in creation, creation of the world, and the immanence or transcendence of God in Islam.

God's Goal in Creation

On the primary point of the necessity of a goal in actions, there are at least three approaches to this issue. The first approach is that the goal of action is exclusive to contingent dependent beings; action should have a goal in order to perfect their incompleteness. An independent ultimate being—that is, God—does *not* have any goal in His actions. It is the meaning of "God's actions are not justified with purposes." Ash'arite theologians such as al-Taftāzani and al-Jurjāni and the philosopher Suhrawardī went in this way.[2]

The second approach, in contrast, contends that there are goals and benefits in God's actions—not for Himself, because He is rich—but for His creations and servants. The Mu'tazilite and Shi'ite theologians believed in this way.[3] The Qur'ān explicitly denies vain creation: "Did you think We created you in vain, and that you would not be brought back to Us?" (al-Mu'minūn [23]:115).[4] The goal of the creation is worship and service of God: "I created jinn and humankind only to worship Me" (al-Dhāriyāt [51]:56). This verse indicates that the creation has a goal. This goal is the worship of God. In the other verse, just end and recompense are introduced as the goal of creation: "God created the heavens and the earth for a true purpose: to reward each soul according to its deeds. They will not be wronged" (al-Jāthiyah [45]:22).

The third approach belongs to the mainstream of the Muslim philosophers: There is no action without a goal.[5] The goal always refers to the agent and is always the perfection of the agent. The need of an agent to a goal is necessary only in the case of a material agent. In incorporeal agents, the goal is the essence of the agent itself, not something out of it. The inference of this argument is that the goal of God in His actions, including creation, is His transcendent essence—nothing else.

The benefit of the creation could not be the essential goal of God in His creation because the goal should not be lower than the existential level of the agent.

This kind of goal requires the influence of the other on God's will, and that is not accepted in the independent agency of God. There could be no motive in His action except His transcendent essence. The benefit of the others is the accident of the divine actions.

Being is good. God is the source and origin of every good. He emanates existences because their creation is good. Origination of good is God's habit, and He necessitated it to Himself, as "He has taken it upon Himself to be merciful" (al-An'ām [6]:12, 54).

God does not need worship, because He is perfect. God loves His transcendental essence. Worshipping Him is justified in this way or could be the accident of creation. According to a ḥadīth commenting on this verse, worship is the intermediate goal. The ultimate goal is "knowing God" (ma'rifat Allāh).[6]

Creation of the World

In Islamic understanding, the creation of the world was not a one-time action that happened in the past and was finished. creation has been continued, and God is a permanent creator.[7] God admired Himself because of the creation of humanity: "glory be to God, the best of creators!" (al-Mu'minūn [23]:14). "We create humanity in the finest state" (al-Tīn [95]:4). The priority of humanity is because of God's spirit in all human beings. He orders the angels to prostrate to humans because of this spirit in human beings: "When I have fashioned him and breathed My spirit into him, bow down before him" (al-Ḥijr [15]:29–30). This spirit in human beings guides them to the straight path if it is not suppressed by carnal soul or devilish ego. This tendency to the good and knowing God is called primordial disposition or original nature (fitra): "So as a man of pure faith, stand firm in your devotion to the religion. This is the natural disposition God instilled in humanity—there is no altering God's creation—and this is the right religion, though most people do not realize it" (al-Rūm [30]:30).

Among the Muslim scholars, two approaches are taken to questions about the creation of the world. The first approach is to say that God creates ex nihilo: the giving of existence out of non-existence. The second approach is to claim the eternality of the world because matter, motion, and time are concomitant. That is, it is impossible to have time but no matter. The incorporeal world is eternal but is not God. The major distinction between God and His creation is not eternality but the contingency and dependence to God. All beings, be they corporeal or incorporeal, are contingent to God and are dependent on Him. The need of temporal being to Him is temporal, and need of eternal being to Him is eternal. This is the approach of mainstream philosophers and some theologians. However, most of the theologians believed in the creation as ex nihilo. The great Ash'arite theologian al-Ghazālī accused the philosophers, including al-Fārābī and Avicenna, of disbelief because of their notions of the eternality of the world.[8]

No verse in the Qur'ān says explicitly that God created the world out of nothing or non-existence. The theologians focus on the literal meaning of *khalaqa*— the word used most often in the Qur'ān's discourse on creation. For example: "It is He who created the heavens and the earth for a true purpose. On the Day when He says, 'Be,' it will be: His word is the truth. All control on the Day the Trumpet is blown belongs to Him. He knows the seen and the unseen: He is the All Wise, the All Aware" (al-An'ām [6]:73).

But *khalaqa* is also used repeatedly in the Qur'ān to refer to the creation from something such as clay or dust: "In God's eyes Jesus is just like Adam: He created him from dust, said to him, 'Be,' and he was" (Āl 'Imrān [3]:59). It is obvious that creation is in harmony with notions both of ex nihilo and out of something.

Philosophers distinguished between "generation" (*ibdā'*) for incorporeal beings and "creation" (*sun'* or *khalq*) for corporeal beings.[9] They prefer the word "emanation" (*fayd*) in place of "creation." In this Qur'ān verse, both "generation" (*ibdā'*) and "creation" (*khalq*) are used: "He is far higher than what they ascribe to Him, the Creator of the heavens and the earth! How could He have children when He has no spouse, when He created all things, and has full knowledge of all things?" (al-An'ām [6]:100b–101). The only Qur'ān verse in which *sun'* is used is this: "You will see the mountains and think they are firmly fixed, but they will float away like clouds. This is the handiwork of God who has perfected all things. He is fully aware of what you do" (al-Naml [27]:88). In Islam, God is creator or originator—not craftsman.

The Immanence and Transcendence of God in Islam

Islam teaches that God is simultaneously nearby His creation and far away from it. Although He is infinitely exalted above all creation (transcendent), He is also near us, present with us and involved in the world (immanent). However, on the one hand, a few Muslim schools of thought believed in divine anthropomorphism because of their literal understanding of the Qur'ān and Sunna; and a few of other Muslim schools, on the other hand, exaggerated in God's transcendence, denying any sort of immanence on His part. The Muslim mainstream believes, first, in the moderate transcendence and immanence of God—God's *tashbih* and *tanzih*— but, second, strongly rejects incarnation in human or any other form, and, third, rejects pantheism or panentheism as well.

Thus, the mainstream position is that God is present in His creatures; there is no place empty of Him; but His presence is a *transcendental* presence. This is the primary principle of perceiving God: "There is nothing like Him" (al-Shūrā [42]:11). Keeping this primary principle in mind, we may perceive God's presence with His creatures, especially human beings, as these Qur'ān verses attest:

He is the First and the Last; the Outer and the Inner; He has knowledge of all things. (al-Ḥadīd [57]:3)

He is with you wherever you are; He sees all that you do." (al-Ḥadīd [57]:4b)

We created man—We know what his soul whispers to him: We are closer to him than his jugular vein. (Qāf [50]:16)

Believers, respond to God and His Messenger when he calls you to that which gives you life. Know that God comes between a man and his heart, and that you will be gathered to Him. (al-Anfāl [8]:24)

As these verses make clear, from an Islamic point of view, God is with each one of His creatures, nearer to them than their jugular vein, between them and their hearts, nearer to them than they are to themselves—but in His glory and majesty, and His transcendence.

Among the verses in the Qur'ān related to immanence is this one about the breathing the spirit of God in human: "You Lord said to the angels, 'I will create a man from clay. When I have shaped him and breathed My Spirit into him, kneel down before him'" (Ṣād [38]:71–72). "Breathing His spirit" means the origination of the incorporeal soul. Human beings have this ability to follow God and run toward Him. Related to this are several clear ḥadīths from 'Alī bin Abī Ṭālib:[10]

"He is with everything, not through association (*muqāranah*)."

"He is other than everything, not through separation (*muzayalah*)."

"To know Him is to profess His unity; and professing His Unity is to distinguish Him (*tamyiz*) from His creation."

"The standard (*hukm*) for distinguishing is separation (*baynunah*) in attribute, not separation in terms of distance (*uzlah*)."[11]

None of the classical Muslim theologians and philosophers perceived God's "withness" (*ma'iyyat*) and presence as divine immanence in the sense of *incarnation* or *pantheism* or *panentheism*. There is unanimity on this point among the Muslim scholars to this day.

The Dignity and Task of Humankind within God's Creation

In this section I discuss three issues: the major point of dignity of humankind, the nature of vicegerency, and the question of whether vicegerency belongs to the individual or to the community.

The Major Point of Dignity of Humankind

"We have honored the children of Adam" (al-Isrā' [17]:70). Humankind has dignity because God breathed into him of His spirit and bestowed on him the primordial disposition or original nature (*fitra*). Humankind because of this advantage was honored with the position of stewardship or vicegerency (*khilāfa*). This vicegerency was not exclusive to Adam but to the children of Adam—that is, humankind: "your Lord told the angels, 'I am putting a vicegerent on earth'" (al-Baqara [2]:30). This verse is about Adam, but according to three other verses—"It is He made you vicegerents on the earth" (Fāṭir [35]:39; al-Anʿām [6]:165; Yūnus [10]:14)—the term *vicegerent* is plural, not singular, and thus includes all of humanity. All of these four verses are talking about the same issue: vicegerency of humanity on the earth. As the Qurʾān speaks of it, "earth" is not exclusive to our specific planet; rather, "earth" means *ʿālam al-shahāda*—the visible or the material world.

Although the majority of Muslim scholars interpreted the story of creation in a factual frame, it seems that it is symbolic regarding some deep transcendental facts. The clearest evidence of this symbolic language is the verse of Trust, which focuses on this exact issue: "We offered the Trust to the heavens, the earth, and the mountains, yet they refused to undertake it and were afraid of it; humanity undertook it—they have always been inept and foolish" (al-Aḥzāb [33]:72). It is obvious that the offer of God to the heavens, the earth, and the mountains was symbolic, as was this offer to humankind. What was this Trust? There is no doubt that it was that vicegerency. It means that humankind's vicegerency on the earth is God's vast Trust. No creature in the visible world except humankind was able to undertake a Trust of this enormity. Humankind did not know the magnificence and difficulty of this Trust in the beginning; nevertheless, they undertook it.

The Nature of Vicegerency

Two factors in humankind prepared it to undertake this enormous Trust: first, humankind's knowledge, and second, his choice. The first factor is mentioned in the story of creation: "And He taught Adam the names of all things" (al-Baqara [2]:31). It is clear that "the names of all things" is the symbol of inherent knowledge in humankind's original nature (*fitra*). Although all human beings have the ability and potentiality to actualize the vicegerency (God's vast Trust), human beings have choice and free will by which to accept or reject it in practice. Humanity's free will is mentioned in the Qurʾān repeatedly.

"By the soul and how He formed it and inspired it [to know] its own rebellion and piety! The one who purifies his soul succeeds and the one who corrupts it fails" (al-Shams [91]:7–11). Here again is mention of God's breathing of His spirit into humankind and bestowing on humanity its original nature (*fitra*). It means that human beings have the choice to undertake the Trust and purify their souls and go in the right path, which will be the actualization of the vicegerency; or they may corrupt their souls, ignore their original nature, and turn their back to God. It is clear that persons who make the latter choice are not God's vicegerents until they repent and return to Him. "We created man from a drop of mingled fluid to put him to the test; We gave him hearing and sight; We guided him to the right path, whether he was grateful or not" (al-Insān [76]:2–3). The Qur'ān explicitly describes the free will of humankind in the story of creation. God showed both the straight path and perversion. Those who are grateful and choose the straight path are actually God's vicegerents, and those who go astray and are ungrateful are not actually God's vicegerents until their return and repentance.

God's purpose in bestowing vicegerency is the perfection of man in the process of creation of the body, breathing the spirit, original nature, knowledge, guidance, showing the good and evil, testing, and finally human choice. The perfection will be the achievement of the soul choice, that is, the straight way. It is the goal of creation in the other verses; I mean worship or knowledge as in tradition. In other words, this purpose could be spiritual meeting with God, and annihilation (al-fanā') in His love and pleasure. This is the station (maqām) of perfection.

"[But] you, soul at peace: return to your Lord well pleased and well pleasing; go in among My servants; and into My Garden" (al-Fajr [89]:27–30). This heaven is more than a material garden; it is God's pleasure. This is the supreme felicity: "God has promised the believers, both men and women, Gardens graced with flowing streams where they will remain; good, peaceful homes in Gardens of lasting bliss; and—greatest of all—God's good pleasure. That is the supreme triumph" (al-Tawba [9]:72).

There is a tight relationship between creation and vicegerency, on one hand, and test (al-ibtilā') and perfection, on the other hand. This world is the time of testing, and the other world is the time of result. Testing is for the purification and perfection of humanity. It is not for increasing the knowledge of God. He is omniscient. Human suffering is because of this big test. Life in one of its meanings is the taking of this test. "Exalted is He who holds all control in His hands; who has power over all things; who created death; who created life to test you and reveal which of you performs best—He is the Mighty, the Forgiving" (al-Mulk [67]:1–2). One of God's goals in the creation of life and death is a test. This test is for purification and perfection that is tied to human deeds. Which of you is best in deed?

Life in this world is mixed with suffering. "We have created humankind for toil and trial" (al-Balad [90]:4). This world does not have capacity for real happiness. The real happiness is the result of two elements: sound faith and good deeds. Both are required for salvation. Neither sound faith without good deeds nor good deeds without sound faith would lead to real happiness and salvation. Human action has a very large role in vicegerency. "Every soul is held in pledge for its deeds" (al-Muddaththir [74]:38). The message of this verse is among the most beautiful of this kind in the Qur'ān: "good words rise up to Him and He lifts up the righteous deed" (Fāṭir [35]:10). "Good words" demonstrate sound faith, in other words, believing in God and believing in the Hereafter: "The believers, the Jews, the Christians, and the Sabians—all those who believe in God and the Last Day and do good—will have their rewards with their Lord. No fear for them, nor will they grieve" (al-Baqara [2]:62). This phrase "those who believe and do good" is used in the Qur'ān repeatedly; for example, "As for those who believe and do good deeds—We do not let the reward of anyone who does a good deed go to waste" (al-Kahf [18]:30).

Vicegerency: Individual or Community?

Undoubtedly individuals and communities are both responsible for their deeds in this world, and both of them will be asked about what they have done in the Day of Judgment. Vicegerency and the responsibility of individuals in general are clear. Here the Qur'ān mentions the responsibility of individuals in relation to creation and the Day of Judgment:

> [God will say], "Now you return to Us, alone, as We first created you: you have left behind everything We gave you, nor do We see those intercessors of yours that you claimed were partners of God. All the bonds between you have been severed, and those about whom you made such claims have deserted you." (al-An'ām [6]:94)

Another clear indication of individual responsibility is this:

> Has he not been told what was written in the Scriptures of Moses and Abraham who fulfilled his duty: that no soul shall bear the burden of another; that a human being will only have what he has worked towards; that his labour will be seen and that in the end he will be repaid in full for it; that the final goal is your Lord." (al-Najm [53]:36–42)

Each human being is responsible for his or her deeds individually. This individuality will be the main aspect of creation, resurrection, and vicegerency.

The membership of a human being in a family or community does not negate this individuality and personality. Those memberships will add new responsibilities to one's major individual responsibility. Family is the second level of responsibility: "Believers, guard yourselves and your families against a Fire fueled by people and stones" (al-Taḥrīm [66]:6a). The third level of responsibility is to one's community: "Be a community that calls for what is good, urges what is right, and forbids what is wrong: those who do this are the successful ones" (Āl 'Imrān [3]:104). We will be asked not only about our deeds but also about our community in the framework of our abilities: "Beware of discord that harms not only the wrongdoers among you: know that God is severe in His punishment" (al-Anfāl [8]:25). In the Day of Judgment both communities and individuals will be called to account: "You will see every community kneeling. Every community will be summoned to its record: 'Today you will be repaid for what you did'" (al-Jāthiyah [45]:28).

But is there any relationship between community responsibility and service as God's vicegerent? Is each community recognized as the vicegerent of God on the earth? It is not clear. I analyze the facts that we have in this case. On one hand, the diversity of communities is accepted not only as a fact but also as God's will:

> People, We created you all from a single man and a single woman, and made you into nations and tribes so that you should get to know one another. In God's eyes, the most honored of you are the ones most aware of Him: God is all knowing, all aware. (al-Ḥujurāt [49]:13)

On the other hand, the purpose of this communal pluralism and diversity is an existential test:

> We have assigned a law and a path to each of you. If God had so willed, He would have made you one community, but He wanted to test you through that which He has given you, so race to do good: you will all return to God and He will make clear to you the matters you differed about. (al-Māʾida [5]:48b)

From the third perspective, the community of believers was characterized as a justly balanced community: "We have made you into a just community, so that you may bear witness [to the truth] before others and so that the Messenger may be witness [to it] before you" (al-Baqara [2]:143a). This characteristic is not only a simple label achieved by confession or heritance of its members. It is not achieved except through sound faith and good deeds. The community of believers, because of the faith and good deeds of its members, will be the witnesses over the communities. This is a spiritual witness and example, nothing else. Although it is possible to equate this spiritual witness with service as God's vicegerent, there is no evidence in the Qur'ān or tradition of this equivalence. *Maqām* of spiritual witness in the Qur'ān is different and separate from *maqām* of vicegerency.[12] The former includes God; the latter is exclusive to humankind individually. There is no evidence of community vicegerency in the Qur'ān.

In our day and age, the exercise of vicegerency in a religiously and ideologically plural world is not different from the exercise of religion per se. The concept of vicegerency does not depend on the premodern era; thus, it need not be changed in the modern era. It is a matter of spirituality and does not deal with this religion or that ideology. It is about truth, not labels. It is about the real faith of heart and dispositions, not the claims of the tongue. Diversities of religions and ideologies that occur in this realm demonstrate that vicegerency is much higher than it. Vicegerency and pluralism do not conflict with each other, because they are not on the same level. The essence of vicegerency is to be understood—as was made clear in Sūrat al-Baqara (2):62, above—as sound faith in God and the Last Day, and righteous deeds regardless of religion and ideology.

Human Action within the Sovereignty of God

Human action and free choice in relation to God's omniscience, omnipotence, and omnibenevolence has been a controversial subject in Abrahamic religions in general, and in relation to the unity of Divine acts (*al-tawḥīd al-ʾafʿālī*) in Islamic thought specifically. There are three subtopics to be considered here: elaboration of God's attributes, notions of moderate human free choice, and classification of verses on the doctrine of mediation between determinism and delegation.

Elaboration of God's Attributes

With regard to discussion of God's attributes, four key problems must be addressed. First, if God knows everything that can be known, He knows human acts before they occur; this leads to determinism because humans are not able to act outside Divine providence and omniscience. Second, if God can do everything that is plausible, there would be no role for human choice in the full omnipotence of God. Any role for human will would mean shortcoming in the sovereignty of God. Third, if there is no ground for human free choice, human sin and committal of evil is not consistent with God's omnibenevolence. Fourth, believing in the notion of unity of Divine acts (*al-tawḥīd al-ʾafʿālī*) requires negation of any kind of non-divine causality, including agency of human action. There is no ground for human free choice, according to this understanding of the unity of God.

These problems arose from an anthropomorphic understanding of God's attributes, weakness in philosophical foundations, and literal interpretation of the scripture and tradition. However, they are resolved by recalling that God's knowledge does not have our restrictions. God does not have mind. His knowledge is not conceptual or empirical knowledge through imprinted forms. His knowledge is knowledge by presence (*al-ʿilm al-ḥuḍūrī*). There is nothing absent from Him. His knowledge is divided into knowledge before and knowledge after the generation of created things. God is omniscient. But His full knowledge does not lead to determinism. Human existence, what is in the human mind, human choice, and action are in God's transcendental presence. God's transcendental knowledge of human choice and mind does not impose any restriction on human freedom. These restrictions are the consequence of our finite knowledge, not God's transcendental infinite knowledge:

> In whatever matter you may be engaged and whatever part of the Qurʾān you are reciting, whatever work you are doing, We witness you when you are engaged in it. Not even the weight of a speck of dust in the earth or sky escapes your Lord, nor anything lesser or greater: it is all written in a clear record. (Yūnus [10]:61)

Predestination and destiny (*al-qaḍā' wa'l-qadar*) do not lead to determinism and negation of human free choice, because human free choice is a part of the human essence according to divine predestination and destiny. In other words, God designed the human essence with free choice, while He designed other creatures without it. This free choice is inseparable from human essence. Free will and choice are among the existential originators (*al-mabādi al-wujudiyya*) of the human essence in God's decree. There is no escape from His predestination and destiny. "He is the Originator of the heavens and the earth, and when He decrees something, He says only, 'Be,' and it is" (al-Baqara [2]:117).

Deterministic interpretation was a pre-Islamic misunderstanding that the Qur'ān explained and condemned. "The idolators will say, 'If God had willed, we would not have ascribed partners to Him—nor would our fathers—or have declared anything forbidden'" (al-An'ām [6]:148a). Tyrannical rulers followed this misinterpretation after Islam to justify their rule.

God's omnipotence does not deny human free choice. Human agency is not horizontal and in competition with God's agency. "God is not to be frustrated by anything in the heavens or on the earth: He is all knowing, all powerful" (Fāṭir [35]:44b). Human agency is vertical, and God is in the chain of causes of human act and the cause of causes. Human agency includes free choice.

Moderate Human Free Choice

Muslim philosophers and theologians, regardless of their diversities, are unanimous in their affirmation of God's omniscience, omnipotence, and omnibenevolence and of the unity of Divine acts (*al-tawḥīd al-'af'ālī*). Yet all Muslim philosophers and the mainstream of Muslim theologians believe in some kind of human free choice. The prominent Muslim theologian Muhammad 'Abduh, Egypt's grand mufti in the early twentieth century, commented: "The doctrine of determinism was the idea of a small, extinct range; and the doctrine of the mediation between determinism and absolute free choice has predominated among the Muslims."[13] 'Abduh is correct. Two radical tendencies were marginalized: that of the ultraliteralist determinists and that of the radical rationalist Mu'tazilites who believed in delegation (*al-tafwīḍ*) or absolute human free choice. I focus on the doctrine of the mediation between determinism and delegation as the mainstream Muslim approach in its two versions of moderate human free choice. The first is the theory of acquisition (*kasb*), popular in Ash'arism; the second is the theory of human agency as the secondary cause, popular in the school of justice in Islamic philosophy and Shi'ism.

The main point of the theory of acquisition is the importance of distinguishing between two elements in human action: creation as God's act and acquisition as human act. God directly creates the power, action, and *kasb* within the human subject—which is no more than the receptacle, the place (*maḥall*), as al-Jurjāni expressed it in his commentary on ʿAḍūd al-Dīn al-Ījī's *al-Mawāqif fī ʿilm al-kalām* (Stations in the Science of Kalām).[14] According to al-Ghazālī, the meaning of acquisition is the creation of a human's action by God at the time of the human's will and power, but there is no effect of the human's power in the creation of his action.[15] The major benefit of this theory is moral responsibility of human as the Ashʿarite scholars expressed. There is no role for the human in his act except synchronization (*al-muqārana*); at the time of generation of power and will in the human, God creates human acts. This synchronization attributes the act to the human as acquisition. Although the theory of acquisition was welcomed by the majority of Ashʿarite theologians, some distinguished Ashʿarite theologians—al-Juwaini, al-Shaʾrani, and Muhammad ʿAbduh among them[16]—denied it as being indistinguishable from determinism.

In support of this position, Ashʿarites refer to this Qurʾān passage: "How can you worship things you carve with your own hands, when it is God who has created you and all your handwork?" (al-Ṣāffāt [37]:95–96). Their argument is based on taking "*ma*" in "*ma taʾmalun*" as *masdariyyah* (infinitive), giving the sense that "God created you and your deeds"—not as *mawsula* (conjunction), giving the sense "God created you and the idols that you carved." According to the context of the verse, the latter interpretation is correct.[17]

Another verse, "People, remember God's grace towards you. Is there any creator other than God to give you sustenance from the heavens and earth?" (Fāṭir [35]:3), denies that there is a creator independent of God, but pagans understood the exclusiveness of any creator, regardless of whether it is independent or contingent (including human agency in its acts). The Qurʾān makes clear that creation by human beings is acceptable, with God's permission: "I have come to you with a sign from your Lord: I will make a bird for you out of clay, then breathe into it and, with God's permission, it will become a real bird; I will heal the blind and the leper, and bring the dead back to life with God's permission" (Āl ʿImrān [3]:49a). So there is no problem with human agency in human creative actions taken with permission of God.

The second theory takes a mediating position between determinism and delegation (*madhab al-amr bain al-amrain*). This position is based on several philosophical principles. Its first principle is that, aside from God, all beings are contingent beings in all of their affairs and their actions. The relationship between cause and effect in precise elaboration is the relationship between creatures that are needy (such as humans) and the One who is rich, God. The contingency, or dependence, or need is not something added to a creature's being. Rather, in its essence, this being per se is needy and is contingent to its transcendent cause. This is the deep meaning of this verse: "People, it is you who stand in need of God—God needs nothing and is worthy of all praise" (Fāṭir [35]:15).

There is no doubt about the unity of Divine acts (*al-tawḥīd al-ʾafʿālī*); but this does not necessitate occasionalism. Although independent origination is exclusive to God, the causality of contingent beings is possible, dependent on God's permission and providence. Human action is not independent of God. On the one hand, it is needy and contingent on God in its being and essence, and, on the other hand, it is impossible to deny or neglect the causality of human action. Human action is attributed to God and humans from two considerations. It is not correct to say it is exclusively God's act, so there is no effect from the human side except the receptacle, the place (*maḥall*); however, it is not solely human action, because both the human agent and his action are always needy and contingent on God. Human beings are the agent of their acts, and simultaneously their acts are God's acts. There is no conflict between these two causalities, because they are in the vertical causes—God is the cause of causes.

The object of God's will is human beings with their free choices, regardless of what they choose—not human beings without choice. Evil human acts do not pose a problem for this analysis because, first, the world is dominated by good; minor evil, which is not an essential object of God, is required as the consequence of the material world, within the context of prevalence of the good. Second, the whole of existence as such is good; evil is relative to specific situations and cannot be attributed to God. All we know under the name of evil is evil accidentally. It means that what is outwardly evil is not evil in its essence, and that essence is attributed to God. God is omnibenevolent; He is the origin of any good: "Anything good that happens to you is from God; anything bad is ultimately from yourself. We have sent you as a messenger to people; God is sufficient witness" (al-Nisā' [4]:79).

Classification of Verses on Doctrine of Mediating Between Determinism and Delegation

There are three groups of verses related to the doctrine of mediating between determinism and delegation that should be read in relation to each other and not separately.[18]

Group One: Verses that indicate that nothing happens except by God's will, providence, and permission. This group negates the doctrine of delegation (*tafwīḍ*). Examples are "But you will only wish to do so by the will of God, the Lord of all people" (al-Takwīr [81]:29) and "Say, 'I have no control over benefit or harm, even to myself, except as God may please'" (al-Aʿrāf [7]:188a).

Group Two: Verses that indicate human free choice and negate determinism, such as

Whoever does good does it for his own soul and whoever does evil does it against his own soul; your Lord is never unjust to His creatures (Fuṣṣilat [41]:46);

Say, "Now the truth has come from your Lord: let those who wish to believe in it do so, and let those who wish to reject it do so" (al-Kahf [18]:29);

If you are ungrateful, remember God has no need of you, yet He is not pleased by ingratitude in His servants; if you are grateful, He is pleased [to see] it in you. No soul will bear another's burden. You will return to your Lord in the end and He will inform you of what you have done: He knows well what is in the depths of [your] hearts (al-Zumar [39]:7); and

Serve God, be mindful of Him and obey me. (al-Insān [76]:3)

Group Three: Verses that indicate two attributes to God and to human beings simultaneously. For example,

It was not you who killed them but God, and when you [Prophet] threw [sand at them] it was not your throw [that defeated them] but God's, to do the believer a favour: God is all seeing and all knowing. (al-Anfāl [8]:17)

Here the Qur'ān has attributed a single act (throwing) to God and to a human being simultaneously. The same thing occurs in other verses: "Fight them: God will punish them at your hands, He will disgrace them, He will help you to conquer them, He will heal the believers' feelings and remove the rage from their hearts" (al-Tawba [9]:14–15a). In a third example, the Qur'ān attributes the same issue to God in one verse and to humanity in another: "Even after that, your hearts became as hard as rocks, or even harder" (al-Baqara [2]:74a[19]); and "But they broke their pledge, so We distanced them [from Us] and hardened their hearts" (al-Mā'ida [5]:13a).

A close reading of verses in the first and second groups indicates that the Qur'ān clearly negates determinism and delegation. Verses in the third group illustrate a core doctrine of the Qur'ān—that is, a position of midway between determinism and delegation (*madhab al-amr bain al-amrain*).

To summarize, in mainstream Islamic thought, the lesson of the Qur'ān is that human action is attributed to God and to the human agent simultaneously. The human agent has free choice in his acts. Human free choice and power are based on God's power, providence, will, and permission. In their existence and in all aspects and affairs of their lives, including their acts, human beings are not independent of God.

Notes

1. For more information, refer to al-Sayyid Muhammad Hussain al-Tabātabā'i, *Nahāytul Hikma* (Ultimate wisdom) (Qom: Mu'assasah al-Nashr al-Islami, 1996).

2. Al-Taftāzani, *Sharhul-Maqāsid*, vol. 2 (Qom: ash-Sharif ar-Radhi, 1989), 156; al-Jurjāni, *Sharh ul-Mawāqif*, vol. 8 (Qom: ash-Sharif ar-Radhi, 1991), 202; and Suhrawardī, *Al-Mutārihat wat-Talwihāt* (Tehran: Anjuman-i Shāhinshāhī-'i Falsafah-'i Īrān, 1977), 437.

3. Nasir ad-Din at-Tussi, *Tajridul I'tiqād*, with commentary of al-Hilli: *Kashul-Murād fi sharh Tajridul I'tiqād* (Qom: Mu'assasah al-Nashr al-Islami, 1996), 422.

4. This and all quotations from the Qur'ān are according to M. A. S. Abdel Haleem, *The Qur'ān: A New Translation* (Oxford: Oxford University Press, 2004).

5. Avicenna, *The Metaphysics of Healing*, trans. Michael Marmura (Provo, UT: Brigham Young University Press, 2005).

6. From an authoritative ḥadīth of Hussain ibn Ali ibn Abi-Tālib, in *Tafsir Nur al-Thaqalain*, vol. 5 (Tehran: Isma'iliyan, 1994), 132.

7. Mulla Ṣadrā, *Risālatu Ḥudūth al-ʿĀlam* [Recital of the Creation of the world] (Tehran: Bunyad-e Islami-e Hikmat-e Sadra, 1999).

8. Refer to Al-Ghazālī, *Incoherence of Philosophers*, trans. Michael Marmura (Provo, UT: Brigham Young University Press, 2002); and Averroes, *Incoherence of Incoherence*, trans. Michael Marmura (Provo, UT: Brigham Young University Press, 2000).

9. Refer to Avicenna, *Remarks and Admonitions: Physics* and *Metaphysics*, trans. Shams C. Inati (New York: Columbia University Press, 1996).

10. The son-in-law of the Prophet, his cousin, the fourth Righteous Caliph and first Shi'ite Imam.

11. William C. Chittick, trans., *A Shi'ite Anthology*, selected by Sayyid Muhammad Husayn Tabataba'i (London: Muhammadi Trust of Great Britain and Northern Ireland, 1979).

12. *Maqām* means spiritual, mystical, or moral station, state, stage, abode, or position.

13. Muhammad 'Abduh, *Risālat hal nahnu mussayyarun am mukhayyarun?* [Are we determined or offered free choice?] 11, reported by Ja'far Sobhani, *al-Ilahiyyat 'ala Huda al-Kitab wa as-Sunnat wa al-'Aql*, by Hassan Muhammad Makki al-'Amili, vol. 2 (Qom: Mu'assasat ul-Imam as-Sadiq, 2009), 262.

14. Al-Jurjāni, *Sharhul-Mawāqif*, vol. 8, 48.

15. Al-Ghazālī, *Al-Iqtisād fi al-I'tiqād* [Mediation in belief] (Cairo: al-Halabi, 1965), 47.

16. Al-Shahrestāni, *al-Milal wa al-Nihal*, vol. 1 (Cairo: al-Halabi, 1967), 98–99; Al-Sha'rāni (Abdul-Wahhab ibn Ahmad), *Al-Yawāqit wa al-Jawahir fi Bayān 'Aqidātel Akabir* (Cairo: al-Halabi, 1959), 139–41; and Muhammad 'Abduh, *Risālat fi al-Tawhid* [A recital on unity of God] (Cairo: Dar ash-Shurouq, 1994), 62–63.

17. Ja'far Subhāni, *al-Ilahiyyat 'ala Huda al-Kitab wa as-Sunnat wa al-'Aql*, by Hassan Muhammad Makki al-'Amili, vol. 2 (Qom: Mu'assasat ul-Imam as-Sadiq, 2009), 283.

18. Ibid., 283–86.

19. See also al-An'ām (6):43, which is similar.

On the Possibility of Holy Living

A Christian Perspective

LUCY GARDNER

> I appeal to you therefore, brethren, by the mercies of God, to present your bodies as a living sacrifice, holy and acceptable to God, which is your spiritual worship. Do not be conformed to this world but be transformed by the renewal of your mind, that you may prove what is the will of God, what is good and acceptable and perfect. (Rom. 12:1–2)

Faced with a task that feels like trying to pack the world into a suitcase, I have deliberately decided not to attempt a hurried historical overview of Christian disagreements about the nature of our existence—and our freedom, in particular. Instead, I offer a brief personal theological guide to negotiating the thematic landscape from one particular Christian point of view. This touches upon Christian beliefs about the person of Christ (the doctrines of the Incarnation and the Trinity, in particular), which cannot be fully explored here. It is, however, my hope that these reflections will demonstrate something of the ways in which these beliefs and doctrines work in relation to other themes.

Creation: Learning to See the World

> In the beginning God created the heavens and the earth. . . . God said "Let there be . . ."; and there was. . . . And God saw that it was good. God said "Let . . ."; and it was so. . . . And God saw that it was good. (from Genesis 1:1–25[1])

The Christian doctrine of Creation is about learning to see and understand the world (that is, the whole universe and everything that is) in the light of its constitutive relationship with God. It is therefore not just about our beginnings and where we come from but about the ongoing characteristics of our existence as created beings who are part of a created whole. In this, however, God remains utterly different from the creation. The relationship between Creator and creation is always asymmetric; it can be guessed at from contemplation of the world itself, but it is, for Christian thought, only fully revealed in God's revelation. Divine revelation happens in creation and in human lives, but for Christianity it happens especially in the life of Israel and in Israel's relationships with her scriptures, and in the life of Christ, in the life of the Church, and in the Church's relationship with scripture. Christian accounts of creation therefore make explicit use of a wide range of scriptures, from both the New and the Old Testament, but always reading them with and in Christ and the Church.[2]

In the Christian understanding, the one, true, and only God, who is the God of Abraham, and Isaac, and Jacob, and the God of Jesus Christ, is the God and creator of all that is. Nothing but God precedes the creation—an insight which is usually described as the doctrine of the Creation ex nihilo. The free God freely creates, and in so doing creates a free world. Likewise, the good God creates a good world. Most importantly of all, the God who is love creates the world in love, out of love, and for love:[3] to be loved by God and to love God in return. This divine act of creation is an ongoing event, and the God who creates the world is also the God who redeems and saves the world—and ultimately the God who sanctifies it. Thus, in being what it is, the world reveals both something of God's nature and something of God's purpose. In all of this the world gives glory to God without in any way adding anything to God.

> In the beginning was the Word, and the Word was with God, and the Word was God. He was in the beginning with God; all things were made through him, and without him was not anything made that was made. In him was life. . . . To all who received him . . . he gave power to become children of God. . . . And the Word became flesh and dwelt among us, full of grace and truth, we have beheld his glory, glory as of the only Son from the Father. (from John 1:1–14[4])

For Christians, this one God is Trinity, and the act of creation is itself Trinitarian; from very early on in Christian responses to Jesus, he is recognized as being an embodied presence of God's Word in the world. He is therefore also puzzlingly understood to have had a part in creation; somehow he was there in the beginning, with God, not just present at creation but active in the divine life and the act of creation, not as a proto-creature himself, nor as another God, but in some sense as part of the one true God. As God's Word, he is part of God, at one with God, not different from God, but not all of God. Likewise, when Christians read the Genesis accounts, we see not only God's creative Word but also God's creative Holy Spirit separately but conjointly at work.

Human Being: Creature of Contradictions

> Then God said, "Let us make man in our image, after our likeness. . . .
> So God created man in his own image, in the image of God he created
> him: male and female he created them. And God blessed them. . . .
> And God saw everything that he had made, and behold, it was very
> good. (from Genesis 1:26–31)

> The Lord God formed man of the dust from the ground, and breathed
> into his nostrils the breath of life; and man became a living being. . . .
> Then the Lord God said, "It is not good that the man should be alone;
> I will make him a helper fit for him. . . . So the Lord cause a deep
> sleep to fall upon the man, and while he slept he took one of his ribs
> and closed up its place with flesh; and the rib which the Lord God had
> taken from the man he made into a woman and brought her to the
> man. Then the man said, "This at last is bone of my bones and flesh
> of my flesh." (from Genesis 2:18–23)

Within God's good creation there are many creatures: particular things, each
with its own particular existence gifted it by God, each sharing general existence
with all the others, without in any proper sense "possessing" it. From among
God's good creatures, "human being" stand out as different, we occupy a particular station; we are endowed with a particular purpose that springs from a different relationship with God. There are two accounts in Genesis of the creation of
human beings. Both mark out a relationship for this creature that is somehow
closer to God than for the other animals and that places the human being in some
sense over against the rest of the world.

This difference from other creatures is worked out in Christian theology as
the doctrine of the image—the *imago Dei*—echoing God's words from Genesis
1:26: "Let us make man in our image, after our likeness." There have been many
different understandings of where and how we are to find this image. Our rationality, our self-awareness, our morality, our religiosity, our language, and our use
of tools have all been suggested as candidates, but most of them are to be found
elsewhere in the creation, if not among the visible animals then in the less visible
realms. One purpose of the image, however, seems to be to indicate the structure
of human existence, describing not a particular faculty nor a part of us but a
particular series of relationships within which we exist. In indicating these, it
then also indicates the purpose within which and the vocation for which we are
made.

For Christian thought, human beings are created out of, in, and for a particular
intimacy with God. To describe this intimacy, this proximity, as an image—that
is, as an icon—suggests that we have a representative role: if we are an icon of
God, then we are not that for God, nor merely for ourselves and each other, but in

some sense for the whole of creation, and therefore for all the other creatures. Genesis makes the point that the image is expressed in the sexual differentiation of "human being" into male and female: only together are they the image. Our sexual differentiation exists not only for our reproduction but in order that we should not be lonely: God says of Adam before the creation of Eve "It is not good that the man should be alone." We are then made a social complexity, for love and companionship, with each other and with God.

Human beings also share in God's creative power of speech. Adam names all the other creatures, and the first couple are particular recipients of God's blessing. This means human beings are creatures who can respond to God in a very particular way. Just like the other creatures, humans are commanded to be fruitful; but unlike the other creatures, we are explicitly given dominion over and responsibility for the other creatures. We are also given a prohibition: not to eat from the fruit of the tree in the midst of the Garden of Eden. Importantly, in this we can see that we are given free will and that this might be part of our difference from some other creatures. We are given positive and negative injunctions, and with them we are given the choice, the freedom, and the ability to obey or disobey them; this is the structure of our freedom.

Notoriously, in and from our first parents onward, we fail in this; we fall away from the path God has set before us—a path that has shape and direction but that is also open to many different expressions. Lamentably, our will is weak and misguided; our understanding is clouded and willful; instead of obeying, we sin.[5] The human being, then, is a puzzle to itself and a frustrating contradiction; but this contradiction is sharpened in the light of the dizzying destiny held out for human being in the rest of scripture.

> Before I formed you in the womb I knew you, and before you were
> born I consecrated you; I appointed you a prophet to the nations.
> . . . See I have set you this day over nations and over kingdoms.
> (Jeremiah 1:5, 10[6])

In Israel, human beings are marked out to be and become not only God's representatives but also God's messengers; not only God's subjects but also God's children; not only God's stewards but also God's lover and bride. Israel receives the gift of God's Word and is entrusted with it for the nations; Israel becomes a partner in and a recipient of God's creative, redemptive, and sanctifying work. But as Israel's apparent privilege increases, so does her responsibility, and with that her predicament and her sense of failure. Her history is a lesson in her own failure and faithlessness, met always by God's persistent faithfulness. She persists as God's People because of God's involvement, because of God's plan, because of God's promises, and because of God's faithfulness to those promises. Hers is a life created, determined, and preserved by covenant with God, and her history is a lesson in the need to rely on God and not herself.

God has highly exalted him and bestowed on him the name that is above every name, that at the name of Jesus every knee should bow, in heaven and on earth and under the earth, and every tongue confess that Jesus Christ is Lord, to the glory of God the Father. (Philippians 2:9–11)

Israel's destiny also contains within it the destiny of humanity as a whole because Israel has a representative role in and to the nations, which mirrors humanity's representative role in and to the world. For Christian belief, this destiny is preeminently fulfilled in the life of Christ and the Church. In the New Testament the theme of the image is taken up and applied to Christ, used to describe the particular relationship that, as God's Son, Christ enjoys with God the Father.[7] Human beings were made in the image of God; Jesus, on the other hand, is the image of God: he is the image in whom we are made; he is also the image in whom we are remade.

The idea of the image is also inked in the New Testament to recognition of Christ's incarnation, his being present as a presence of God's Word in the world as a human being. It is therefore also linked to his involvement in the creation itself and to his connection with the rest of humanity. Similarly, the theme of dominion also transfers to Christ. He is given dominion over all things and is exalted above the whole of creation by God the Father.[8] In numerous New Testament texts, he is both instrumental in and the reason for the creation of all worldly powers.[9] But, importantly, Christ does not receive these things in any sense "for himself." He also takes up the representative role of human being and Israel. He receives all this, as it were, on our behalf. In him, all of humanity also receives them. As he receives them, and as others become united to him, they—and, ultimately, the whole of creation—also enjoy them and can come to enjoy what St. Paul, in Romans 8:21, evocatively calls "the glorious liberty of the children of God." In Christ, humanity, our human nature, our human existence, is itself transformed and fulfilled; in him each one of the human race can likewise be transformed and fulfilled.

Human Freedom: Virtue, Creativity, and the Possibility of Holy Living

If all this outlines for us our "vocation" (what we are called to be) and our "condition" (that and why we fail at that, and that God has provided the means for overcoming this fact in Israel and Christ), then how are we called to act and behave in the world? And what is the nature, the character, the quality of any of our actions in relation to God's absolute sovereignty, on the one hand, and our divinely given freedom, on the other? Is there not a perpetual problem that one of these will cancel out the other?

Our Lord Jesus Christ said:

> Hear, O Israel, the Lord our God is one Lord;
> and thou shalt love the Lord thy God with all thy heart,
> and with all thy soul, and with all thy mind,
> and with all thy strength.
> This is the first commandment.
> And the second is like, namely this:
> Thou shalt love thy neighbour as thyself.
> There is none other commandment greater than these.
> On these two commandments hang all the law and the prophets.
> **Lord, have mercy upon us,**
> **and write all these thy laws in our hearts, we beseech thee.**[10]

The Old Testament, and the prophets in particular, are clear on two interconnected points: human beings have some knowledge of good and evil, but they also require God's specific guidance to live a good life. This guidance is generously given by God in the law with its interconnected divine commands to worship God, to love and respect one another, and to work for peace and justice throughout the created order. Part of Israel's vocation is to receive and treasure these commands for the world and to keep them on its behalf. Far from casting these commands aside, Christ comes to enact Israel's law perfectly in his life, to fulfill it and in some sense complete it; the interconnection of the God-ward laws and the creation-ward laws, so often underscored by the prophets, is reemphasized by Christ's life and teaching. Insofar as Christ does give his followers any "new commandments," they are never flat contradictions of the Jewish law but rather a profound intensification of them, and his most famous "new commandment" is that the disciples should love one another just as he has loved them.

It should be obvious how human beings are meant to behave: we are to love God; we are to love one another, even our enemies; and we are to care for the earth. This is the particular part we are given to play in creation's general purpose of giving glory to God. In its account of sin, however, the Christian faith is equally insistent that every single one of us, including the saints, has in some sense failed in this task, "for all have sinned and fall short of the glory of God" (Romans 3:23). This is because of our sinful exercise of our free will. Human beings experience an in-built tendency to sin, which is not part of our nature but which is nevertheless very real. This means that we do not fulfill God's law nor can we rescue ourselves from our predicament. It seems that the law by itself is insufficient for us, and our divinely granted freedom is more a curse than a blessing.

The history of Israel's battle with her vocation in the Old Testament, however, shows that, in addition to the two gifts of our freedom and the divine law, God also supplies a third gift, that of divine grace, to assist us in exercising the one (our freedom) and in fulfilling the other (the law). By God's grace, because of God's creative Word and God's faithfulness to that Word, and not on any merit of her own, Israel remains the Chosen People, despite her wanton faithlessness; as, for example, the story of Joseph shows, God works with Israel's history to turn even her faithlessness into the occasion and means for her purification. But if sin defeats us and grace assists us, are we really "free"? Are we not rather caught between competing forces, tossed on waves over which we have no power? As theologian Howard McCabe puts it,

> I am free in fact, not because God withdraws from me and leaves me my independence—as with a man who frees his slaves, or good parents who let their children come into independence—but just the other way round. I am free because God is in a sense more directly the cause of my actions than he is of the behaviour of unfree beings. In the case of an unfree creature its behaviour is perhaps its own (in the case of a living thing—for this is what we mean by a living thing), but it is also caused by what gave it its structure and whatever forces are operating on it. . . . God does bring about the action of the dog, but he does so by causing other things to cause it. God brings about my free action, however, not by causing other things to cause it, he brings it about directly. The creative act of God is there immediately in my freedom.[11]

First, we must not mistake our God-given freedom and independence with radical but rebellious versions of them. Human freedom is not (ultimately) just to do whatever we want. It is quite simply nothing other than the freedom to choose between two modes of being and doing: to accept and work with God's will or to reject it. This means that our freedom "to do what we want" is indeed in a sense only a "limited" freedom, but this is a consequence of our intended greater freedom: to become what God has always intended us to be—that is, willing, free participants in God's great loving project of creation, redemption, and sanctification—and therefore ultimately in God's life itself. Within this we are offered, and as creative creatures we are able to create for ourselves, an infinite variety of ways to work with God and God's will—and likewise we can make an infinite variety of ways to reject God—as literature, history, and the lives of the saints show.

Second, we must understand that God's grace, the divine assistance, is not an additional, subsequent divine "intervention" or "interference" in the created order, nor is it a means by which God in fact surreptitiously limits our freedom. It is part of the free, creative divine love, and it is a free divine gift; it is both given to creatures at their creation and subsequently bestowed upon them not as an afterthought nor merely in response to creaturely actions but as part of the planned, ongoing divine, creative initiative within the creation as well as the involved, redemptive, and sanctifying interplay with it. The Creator is free; the creation is both utterly dependent and genuinely free as a result of the free divine will; anything that happens within the world is always the result of the interaction between these two freedoms.

> The Lord is not slow about his promise as some count slowness, but is forbearing toward you, not wishing that any should perish, but that all should reach repentance. (2 Peter 3:9)

At first glance the Christian doctrine of redemption appears to offer an even greater stumbling block to an assertion of our freedom than the doctrine of Creation: even if grace is not to be read as "interfering," isn't there a sense in which redemption can be seen precisely as God trying to overrule or cancel out our freedom? Christian faith, firmly grounded in numerous verses of scripture as in its overarching story as a whole, insists that the redemption offered in Christ is consonant with and indeed a part of God's eternal plan and God's good providence.

Here I consider two "limit cases" (in each of which the whole of humanity is represented) as demonstration of the Christian understanding that God's foreknowledge (precisely of our sin) and our "predestination" are themselves freeing rather than limiting. First, there is the problem of Christ's executors. If Christ's crucifixion was in some sense part of God's plan all along, as the Bible clearly argues, doesn't this undercut the freedom of his executors? Do they not become ghastly puppets who exercise a merely illusory freedom in a gruesome drama? The mystery of salvation offered in Christ is that his execution is indeed a free human act, even though it is influenced by sin and evil. The Father does not kill the Son; human beings do. This is nothing other than "pure" sin; it is the actual enactment of the greatest possible depth and summit of human rejection of God and God's love. God, however, foresees—foreknows, even—this act of rebellion and makes it part of the plan for redemption and the very means of salvation. Even when Jesus appears to be at the mercy of others, he remains the true initiator of the action and the drama not only in consenting to what happens but also in persistently offering himself, his life (and ultimately his death) in love, simultaneously to the Father and to the world (us) as his faithful obedience to the Father's will. He was sent to bring and be God's love for the world in the world. In giving himself to his betrayers and consenting to his own death, he persists in fulfilling the Father's will at every stage. But in this, God subverts every betrayal and separates it from its "natural," "final" end (death) and (in a "wonderful exchange") miraculously makes it the basis for the possibility of sharing, despite those betrayals, in his eternal, resurrection life. This holds for the disciples who betray him as much as for the soldiers who kill him, and it holds for everyone who ever rejects or betrays God and God's good will. Even our worst act (the rejection of God) has its place in the interplay between divine and human freedom and in the outworking of God's good purposes for creation. Far from being evidence of a lack of human freedom, the crucifixion in fact proves the reality and the extent of that freedom: we are able and free to reject God, but this does not limit God's freedom and sovereignty.

But this suggests another question and my second limit case: Will everyone be saved? If so, isn't our freedom limited? If not, isn't God's will frustrated and God's freedom limited? Christian orthodoxy has tended to understand that there are two real possible "futures" (life and death) held before us, futures that will depend on our free choices for or against God and God's will. But it also understands that our intended destiny is life and that we are given the means of reaching this. Simple universalism is rejected, but Christians are required to pray for the salvation of all.[12] This at least suggests the fervent hope that the ultimate outcome of the interplay between divine and human freedom might indeed be that all will be saved. God's desire and freedom will not in any sense be limited by creaturely freedom, on the one hand, nor will God necessarily have to cancel our freedom in order to bring that about, on the other hand; God will patiently wait as long as it takes.

Taken together, therefore, these two limit cases precisely show that neither freedom has to cancel out the other and that God rejects the options that would make this the case.

> O Lord, open thou our lips.
> Answer: **And our mouth shall show forth thy praise.**

> O God, make speed to save us.
> Answer: **O Lord, make haste to help us.**

> Glory be to the Father, and to the Son, and to the Holy Ghost;
> Answer: **As it was in the beginning, is now, and ever shall be, world without end. Amen.**

> Praise ye the Lord.
> Answer: **The Lord's Name be praised.**[13]

In many places the Bible suggests that this interplay between divine and human freedom can be understood as a conversation: God creates the world by speaking, and God addresses it in many ways. Humanity is called to answer on behalf of the whole creation, especially in worshipping God. Since Jesus is the Word of God, then he has an important part in this. His life is God's creative-redemptive, loving "Yes" to creation; he is also God's saving Word of Judgment and God's healing Word of Love. But since Jesus is also fully human, he also gives the human creature's ultimate grateful, obedient, responsive "yes" to God. As the divinely human one, Christ is and does this on our behalf; but he is also the possibility of our giving a grateful, obedient, sufficient, and satisfactory responsive "yes" to God ourselves. In this vein, Christ's whole life (and not merely his death) can be interpreted as a prayer, as true worship, and as sacrifice. He saves us by offering us an offering, the offering that we should give, in which we can participate; but that offering, his life, is not something "new" or "additional" to the life of God; it is part of a conversation, a loving that has existed in God since before the beginning of the world: it is God's own life.

For Christians, then, our response to God is determined by our response to Christ; we shall be judged on how we have "answered" the Word addressed to us in and by him. In particular, we may note here Christ's question to the disciples: "who do you say that I am?" (Matt. 16:15; Mark 8:29; Luke 9:20). To this the Christian answer is free confession, but it is also a confession for which we are provided the script: we confess with St. Peter that Jesus is "the Messiah" and "the Son of the living God" (Matt. 16:16); with St. Thomas we confess that he is "My Lord and my God" (John 20:28); and with the Church we confess that he is "the only begotten Son of God." All of these confessions name Christ, but they also place us in relation to him and to God. Each of them can be spoken in an infinite variety of ways; we have the creative freedom of improvisation and are not tied to mimicry, parody, and mere repetition.

In this way Christ offers the world the opportunity to participate in the eternal conversation that is God's own life. Christian participation in this conversation begins in response to Christ, but it continues in learning to pray with him. At the heart of his letter to the Romans, St. Paul describes the act of Christian prayer thus:

> When we cry, "Abba! Father!" it is the Spirit himself bearing witness with our spirit that we are children of God, and if children, then heirs, heirs of God and fellow heirs with Christ. (from Romans 8: 15–17)

When Christians pray with Christ and in Christ's name, they pray to God the Father, but they also find that it is the power of God, God the Holy Spirit, working in them to help them pray, and this gradually unites them with, grafts them into, the Word of God, God the Son. This means that we cannot simply think of prayer and our human response to God as a two-way interaction or dialogue between us and God, which would in a sense be impossible on account of the asymmetry of the relationship and God's "ever greater dissimilarity" from us. Christian prayer is our being drawn into the preexistent three-way interaction between the three persons of God, which precedes our participation but is offered to us.

As our Saviour Christ hath commanded and taught us, we are bold
to say:

> Our Father who art in heaven, hallowed by thy name.
> Thy kingdom come, Thy will be done, On earth as it is in heaven.
> Give us this day our daily bread;
> And forgive us our debts, As we also have forgiven our debtors;
> And lead us not into temptation, But deliver us from evil.
> For Thine is the Kingdom, the Power and the Glory, for ever and
> ever. Amen. (from the Order for Holy Communion, in the Church
> of England Book of Common Prayer, 1662[14])

When Christ teaches the disciples to pray, he gives them the "Lord's Prayer."
These are not just words to repeat, though Christians have prayed those words
ever since. They form a paradigm for all Christian prayer but also for all Christian life, which can likewise be understood as a growing into participation in
Christ's life as the conversation within God. Jesus Christ is the Word of God; he
is the Word to the Father, but he is also this Word to and for the world. Each
phrase of that Lord's Prayer can be read as the expression of desire—that God
will become "Our Father" as Christ becomes our brother; that God's Name will
be hallowed throughout the creation and in our lives; that God's will will be done;
that God's Kingdom will come; that the essentials of life will be forthcoming
from God for all; that we shall forgive and be forgiven; and that we shall be
delivered from evil. In repeating these petitions with Christ, Christians are taught
to learn to want and work for what God wants; our desires are cleansed and
purified to resonate only with God's Word, with God's good will, and with God's
good purposes. This is what living according to God's good will looks like. It
requires us to place our trust utterly in God; it expects us to participate in bringing that will about and to recognize that we always need to learn what God's will
actually is and how to want it.

   But the Word that Christ is for and to the Father in all eternity, the character
of his prayer, is perhaps best understood not so much as supplication as "thanksgiving": thanksgiving for his own life and existence but thanks also for all that
has been made and given to him—thanksgiving for the whole world. This eternal
thanksgiving is what is offered us as eternal life in heaven; but it is also offered
as something we can begin and enjoy now, in our own prayer lives and in the
Church's liturgy, especially in her celebration of the Eucharist, which is only
another name for Christ's thanksgiving offering. In this, that which is held before
us as our final destiny (heavenly beatitude: eternally worshipping the Father,
with the Son, in the power of the Spirit) is made a reality and a possibility for
human lives here and now. As we pray in resonance with God's Word in Christ,
we become one with him; as his prayer becomes our prayer, we are indeed

transformed. We are conformed to him, becoming ever more truly ourselves and ever more part of his offering to the Father, thus taking up our promised place in the divine life and enjoying what St. Paul called the "glorious liberty of the children of God" (Rom. 8:21).

One of the paradoxes of the Christian revelation, therefore, is that just doing what we want is not really freedom; it is "following too much the devices and desires of our own hearts" and results in bondage to sin.[15] Doing what God wants, on the other hand, is true freedom, resulting in that "glorious liberty of the children of God" and eternal happiness—not only for "human being" but for the whole of creation. True freedom, then, is cooperation with God and God's good purposes; it is to offer our lives in holy service to God. Anything else is sin and slavery. Sin looks like freedom but is in fact slavery. Obedience might look like slavery but is in fact true freedom.

This glorious liberty of the children of God promised to the world in Christ is not, then, merely the freedom to do what we want, with no fear of any consequences, nor the freedom simply to become whatever we choose to be; nor is it even the freedom to live a good life characterized by good decisions, and perhaps therefore punctuated by regular, faithful acts of worship. It is the freedom to embrace the possibility of living a holy life, the life of the saints to which St. Paul reminds the Romans they are called: lives lived as entirely free, personal, grateful offerings to God, within God's own life and action, which for Christians at least is about each of us, assisted by divine grace and empowered by the Holy Spirit, taking up our God-given place within Christ's life, his prayer, his offering, his sacrifice, his eternal Eucharist.

We can, however, never simply "be" or "become" holy; nor can we make ourselves holy. We must be made holy; to be holy is to be set apart by and for God. In our "becoming holy," we need to learn to work with God. At the same time, however, we need to learn that, though God can undoubtedly work "without" us and "despite" us, God chooses to work with us. This sanctification was always God's good intention for humanity and the whole of creation. This adds a final important statement to my summary of the Christian doctrine of Creation: the holy God is creating a world that is becoming holy. Making holy is the purpose, the shape, the structure, and the goal of the exquisite, intricate interplay between the divine and creaturely (specifically human) "freedoms," which are linked but also utterly different. A human life well lived, a holy human life, will always be one that cooperates with divine operation.

Coda: Theology and Ethics

Part of what we are supposed to do (our ethics) is to speak well, truthfully, and faithfully of God; part of our appropriate response to God is "confession," and "theology" has its part to play in that as a human practice, and not merely as one side of a tension or opposition between "thinking" and "doing." But both "theology" (thinking) and "ethics" (doing) spring from the direction in which we choose to face and live our lives, the goal to which we allow ourselves to be drawn (our "orientation" or our "attitude," be that God-ward or otherwise). This is the sense in which liturgy, worship, is prior to and the wellspring of both theology and ethics, just as it is that to which both tend and should be directed; true worship, the divine liturgy, encompasses theology and ethics. It is also the reason for insisting that there are only relative distinctions to be drawn between the different "disciplines" within theology (biblical, systematic, moral, liturgical, etc.) that consider different aspects of our existence and activity. In this view, moreover, Christian theology, together with Christian liturgy and Christian ethics, is not a response to human intuition and insight, nor is it merely a matter of a human response to divine revelation. All three of these are about human participation in divine activity, empowered, engraced by the Spirit. Our talk "about" God (in our theology) can only spring from our conversation "with" God, and our participation "in" the conversation between the Father, the Son, and the Holy Spirit that already exists within God (which happens in our liturgy but is also the ground not only of our spiritual life but for our moral actions). It is not by chance that the thoroughly "theological," Trinitarian, and Christological expositions of Romans 8, 1 John 4, Philippians 2, and Colossians 1 to which I have repeatedly referred all occur as and within unavoidable, explicit moments of confession and worship, and in the middle of exhortations to good and holy living.[16] Nor is it chance (or even merely a particularly "Anglican" quirk) that the sources for my reflections have been taken largely from scriptural and liturgical texts.

Notes

Epigraph: In its rendition of Romans 12:1, the King James Version has "reasonable service" for "spiritual worship"—an alternative that helps to point up the rich resonances of Paul's phrase and the fabric of my argument here, particularly the ways in which worship and service are in some sense the "same" appropriate response to God, and the way in which "spiritual" indicates not only the religious sphere but also the whole intellectual and interior life: that dimension of human existence that is precisely "closest" to God and a regular candidate for the location of the "image of God" that is to be found in human being.

In this essay, all biblical quotations are according to the Revised Standard Version.

1. Equally important for an "Old Testament" understanding of creation are texts such as the Psalms, Isaiah 40–55, Amos 1–3, and Jeremiah 10:11–16, in which we learn that the God of Israel is the God of the whole world and, most particularly, that the God who saves is the God who creates (and the God who creates is the God who saves). Creation and redemption are not two separate "acts" of God occurring in chronological sequence, one after the other. God creates Israel by choosing, calling, sending, and leading them; in rescuing them from slavery in Egypt, God re-creates Israel by again choosing, calling, sending, and leading them, thus both reaffirming and persisting in that "original"

free choice to make a free people. The author of life is also the giver of new life; even from "before" its creation, God desires to save the world.

2. I shall indicate some of Christian theology's grounding in scripture, but lack of space precludes attention to extensive scriptural exegesis here; my task is rather to summarize some of the key points of Christian understanding of creation as they touch upon our themes of human freedom, action, and creativity.

3. For this insight, the Johannine writings (the Gospel of John, and the Letters of John) are particularly key.

4. There are several other key New Testament texts relating Christ to the work of creation, including the opening to the Letter to the Hebrews and the "hymn" of Colossians 1. Verse 16 is particularly important "in him all things were created, in heaven and on earth, visible and invisible" as it can be read as foundational for significant clauses in the Christian creeds: in the first article, God the Father is identified as "maker of heaven and earth, of all things, visible and invisible" and in the second article, of Christ, the Son of God, "through whom all things were made."

5. St. Paul provides helpful and extensive reflections on this lamentable contradiction. See, for example, Romans 7:15–19.

6. This description of the prophet's task in Jeremiah 1 is an example of a particular vocation that can be transferred to Israel as a whole, highlighting that Israel's role among the nations is indeed that of being "sent" to the nations, as prophet, messenger, ambassador, and deeply mining the theme of "fore-ordination." In Christian theology and liturgy, it is also applied to Christ and transferred to the Church as well as to individuals.

7. See, for example, Colossians 1:15–19: "He is the image of the invisible God; . . . in him all the fullness of God was pleased to dwell."

8. See, for example, the Philippians hymn: "God has highly exalted him and bestowed on him the name that is above every name, that at the name of Jesus ever knee should bow, in heaven and on earth and under the earth, and every tongue confess that Jesus Christ is Lord, to the glory of God the Father." Philippians 2:9–11.

9. Again, see, for example, the Letter to the Hebrews and many of the images of the book of Revelation for similar reflections on Christ's exalted humanity and engagement in creation.

10. Church of England, *Common Worship*, Order Two for the Eucharist, at the place where the Western Church has traditionally placed the Confession, reusing material from the proposed 1928 Book of Common Prayer, and quoting Christ's words from Matthew 22:37–40. The main text is read by the minister to the congregation, who then respond by addressing God with the words in bold.

11. Herbert McCabe, "Freedom," in *God Matters* (London: Mowbray, 2000), 14.

12. See 1 Timothy 2, which urges the faithful to make supplications, prayers, intercessions, and thanksgivings "for everyone" (v. 1.) because God "desires everyone to be saved" (v. 4); and 2 Peter 3:9, which explains that God does not wish "that any should perish."

13. These are the words with which the Church of England services of Matins and Evensong (Morning Prayer and Evening Prayer) usually begin; they capture beautifully the dialogic structure of Christian liturgy. The phrases (apart from the doxology "Glory be . . . world without end") are also quotations from scripture and serve to demonstrate the way in which Christian worship is precisely to use God-given words to participate in a preexistent divine "conversation." The content, attitude, and character of these phrases are also illustrative of my theological argument here: to worship God truly and faithfully,

we need God's assistance, but we need to request that assistance, consent to it, give it permission, desire it, and even "instruct" it.

14. This text of what is commonly called "The Lord's Prayer," the "Our Father," or the "Pater Noster," is based on words delivered by Christ to his disciples, when he says to them, "When you pray, pray like this. . . ." See Matthew 6:9–13 and Luke 11:2–4.

15. The words are taken from the Confession in the 1928 Book of Common Prayer's provision for Evensong: "Almighty and most merciful Father; We have erred, and strayed from thy ways like lost sheep. We have followed too much the devices and desires of our own hearts. We have offended against thy holy laws. We have left undone those things which we ought to have done; And we have done those things which we ought not to have done; And there is no health in us. But thou, O Lord, have mercy upon us, miserable offenders. Spare thou those, O God, who confess their faults. Restore thou those who are penitent; According to thy promises declared unto mankind In Christ Jesus our Lord. And grant, O most merciful Father, for his sake; That we may hereafter live a godly, righteous, and sober life, To the glory of thy holy Name. Amen."

16. These three different spheres (theology, ethics, and liturgy) are intimately bound together, and they are so not only in scripture but also in subsequent Christian thought. St. Thomas Aquinas, for example, seeks to teach us as much how to live and behave well as what to think and understand about God; indeed, all his theology is directed to that practical, pastoral purpose and not merely presented as incidental or preparatory information for the task. Similarly, St. Augustine's famous *De Trinitate* is more about coaching his readers in the human journey into divine wisdom and eternal life than about trying to understand the triune nature of God in its own right. This is why his treatment of the doctrine of the image is so important for his argument and purpose: he sees in it an indication of our ability to remember, know, and desire God rather than any capacity simply statically to "represent" God; for him the "image" and the structure of our interior life are our potential to grow ever closer to God. For further thinking in this vein, see, for example, Philip Egan's treatment of both St. Augustine and St. Thomas Aquinas in his *Philosophy and Catholic Theology: A Primer* (Collegeville, MN: Michael Glazier, 2009). See also Lewis Ayres, *Augustine and the Trinity* (Cambridge: Cambridge University Press, 2014) and Ellen T. Charry's attention to St. Augustine in the sixth chapter of her *By the Renewing of Your Mind: The Pastoral Function of Christian Doctrine* (New York: Oxford University Press, 1997).

PART II

God's Creation and Its Goal

God's Creation and Its Goal

A Muslim Perspective

SOHAIRA ZAHID SIDDIQUI

THE QUESTION OF God's Creation and its purpose is a perennial one that has both stumped exegetes of the Qurʾān and caused theologians to be embroiled in intense debates over the centuries. In offering a reflection on this topic, it is important to connect scriptural reflections on specific verses in the Qurʾān to their theological implications throughout Islamic intellectual history. To this extent, personal reflections on verses of the Qurʾān will be tethered to the more technical theological inquiries they contributed to. More specifically, these inquiries are (1) What does the mere presence of creation reveal about God's nature? (2) What obligation does Creation bear toward God? And (3) How can we understand God's continuous creation?

God's Creation and God's Nature

In postulating a theology, the Qurʾān and ḥadīth are seen as the only sources of divine revelation. To define a theology without reference to these two scriptural sources would render the theology inconsequential to Muslims. The distinction between the two sources is that whereas the former is recited revelation (*waḥy maṭlu*), the latter is unrecited revelation (*waḥy ghayr maṭlu*). When engaged in the scholarly investigation of the divine, exegetes and theologians have limited themselves to describing God as He describes Himself; in other words, divine disclosure is limited to direct indications found in the Qurʾān. Muslim scholars are also keen on maintaining a distinction between the finite individual and the infinite God. The result is a theological focus on attributes (*ṣifāt*) God uses within the Qurʾān to refer to Himself.[1]

It is likely that the first theologian to systematically analyze God's attributes was the Muʿtazilite theologian Abū l-Hudhayl (d. 227/841), who quickly realized that thinking of God in terms of attributes could very easily undermine His singularity, which in turn would pose a great theological problem.[2] In one of the most important chapters of the Qur'ān, God supplies Muslims with their foundational theological belief: "Say, 'He is God the One, God the eternal. He fathered no one nor was He fathered. No one is comparable to Him'" (al-Ikhlāṣ [112]:1–4).[3] To maintain the unity of God emphasized in the verse, later Ashʿarī theologians internally settled the debate by arguing that God has one essence but multiple other eternal attributes.[4] For Ashʿarīs, the eight primary attributes of God are power, knowledge, life, will, hearing, sight, speech, and enduringness (baqā'). These primary attributes, taken from the Qur'ān, were simply understood as God's self-disclosure. In other words, they were to be accepted without further questioning or inquiry, referred to as the bi-lā kayf doctrine, literally the "without why" doctrine. What is important is that most of these attributes can also be used to characterize human beings, the one exception being enduringness. The enduringness of God is tied to His eternal nature; He was present in the world *before* creation, and He will endure in the world *after* creation. In this sense, the defining feature of God is His eternality, while the defining feature of man is his temporality. It is within this interplay between eternality and temporality that the question of creation unfolds.

In the Qur'ān, God's eternality and the temporal createdness of everything else in the world can be extracted from the verses describing the process of creation: "They have asserted, 'God has a child.' May He be exalted! No! Everything in the heavens and earth belongs to Him, everything devoutly obeys His will. He is the Originator of the heavens and the earth, and when He decrees something, He says only, 'Be,' and it is" (al-Baqara [2]:116–17). And elsewhere, in the story of Jesus's conception, "She said, 'My Lord, how can I have a son when no man has touched me?' [The angel] said, 'This is how God creates what He will: when He has ordained something, He only says, "Be," and it is" (Āl ʿImrān [3]:47). God says "Be" and "it is" suggests that creation requires nothing but a single divine command.

Interestingly, God says to "it" the creative command, meaning there is an object to His command. The pronoun *hu* (it) refers to *amr*—translated here as "thing," but it can best be understood as something that exists in the imagination of God not yet manifest in the material world. In tracing the creative process, what is abstract in the imagination of God is subject to His creative command, which then manifests itself as a thing. Because it is ultimately a created thing and can perish, it is connected to God by virtue of its coming into existence but disconnected from God as it is inherently temporal.

This process of creation, while revealing something about God's attributes, does not answer the question of why the world is created and what an individual's precise role within in it is. Elsewhere in the Qur'ān, God answers this by saying, "I created jinn and mankind only to worship Me" (al-Dhāriyāt [51]:56). A similar thought is conveyed in a ḥadīth *qudsi*, famously known as the Ḥadīth of the Hidden

Treasure, wherein the Prophet quotes God as saying "I was a hidden treasure [*kanza makhfiyan*] and I desired to be known, so I created the entire created world [*khalq*] so that I may be known."[5] Despite similarities, these two statements of God are not identical. In the Qur'ānic verse, God is noting that the purpose of creation is for humanity to worship Him; while in the Ḥadīth, the purpose of creation is for humanity to come to know God. A potential way to reconcile these two statements is to think of worship as a means of knowing God—by virtue of one's fulfilling one's duty of worship, one will come to know God as He intended Himself to be known.

Humanity's Obligation to God

For Muslim scholars the requirement to know and worship God posed a series of problems: How does the individual come to know this is his or her duty? And if a precondition for worshipping God is believing in God, how does one come to believe in God? And does the duty of worship as established in Sūra 51:56 extend beyond humankind and jinn to all created beings, or is it specific to them?

Starting with the final and arguably easiest question, in several places in the Qur'ān God states that certain modes of creation are constantly in a state of worship and submission: "Everything in the heavens and earth glorifies God, the Controller, the Holy One, the Almighty, the Wise" (al-Jumu'a [62]:1); and "Do you not realize [Prophet] that everything in the heavens and earth bows down to God: the sun, the moon, the stars, the mountains, the trees, and the animals? So do many human beings, though for many others punishment is well deserved. Anyone disgraced by God will have no one to honour him: God does whatever He will" (al-Ḥajj [22]:18). Every animate and inanimate being in these verses is in a state of submission and praise. The Qur'ān personifies inanimate objects such as mountains, stars, and trees and describes their submission as manifest through prostration, glorification, thankfulness, and obedience to God's command.[6] Through these verses it becomes clear that submission and worship to God can either be programmatic or volitional.

Indeed, creation can be grouped according to God's provision of choice to His creation in the following manner. The first is creation that is completely submissive to God, accepts and recognizes its subjugation, and does not question God. These are inanimate objects such as the mountains, stars, and trees. The second is animate creation that is completely submissive to God, accepts and recognizes its subjugation, but has the ability to question God, though not disobey Him. In this grouping are the angels, who, when informed by God of the creation of human beings, responded by asking, "How can You put someone there who will cause damage and bloodshed when we celebrate Your praise and proclaim Your holiness?" (al-Baqara [2]:30). The shock of the angels pivots upon their glorification and sanctification of God and their fear that God's new creation will not be as praiseworthy, implying that the role of creation is submission to and worship of God. God responds by asserting that He is more knowledgeable than the angels; and then, in the Qur'ān, the story of Adam's creation immediately follows. In this exchange between God and the angels, while the angels are perplexed at God's decision, their praise of Him is not suspended. In fact, Qur'ānic scholars argued that it is the *inability* of angels to disobey God that affords them the ability to act as intermediaries between God and humankind and as vessels of divine revelation, as was the case with Gabriel and the Prophet Muhammad.

The third type of creation is also animate but has the choice of being submissive to God or rejecting subjugation. In this category are both jinn and humankind.[7] Focusing more specifically on humankind, after the creation of Adam God says, "you and your wife, Adam, live in the Garden. Both of you eat whatever you like, but do not go near this tree or you will become wrongdoers" (al-A'rāf [7]:19). Adam's free rein was limited only by a single command of God to not approach a specific tree, yet he still transgresses the boundaries set forth by God and approaches the tree. For theologians, this action on the part of Adam signifies that humankind has the ability to willfully accept or reject God's commands and, by extension, believes, as God famously says, "There is no compulsion in religion" (al-Baqara [2]:256). It also establishes that there is no causal link between knowledge of God and continuously worshipping and submitting to God, as arguably Adam had knowledge of God but was still able to sin and disobey. If this is indeed the case, then how does the individual come to know and believe God and then come to choose between worshipping Him and disobeying Him?

The Ash'arī theological school, which came to dominate the Sunnī world by the eleventh century of the common era, argued that belief (*imān*) is defined by assent (*taṣdīq*) and not necessarily obedience (*ṭā'a*). For the Ash'arīs, this was the only way to understand the story of Adam; Adam's disobedience was not a case of disbelief, it was merely disobedience, which does not impact one's actual assent to belief.[8] As they argued, assent refers to belief in God and the veracity of the Prophetic message, entailing belief in both the Qur'ān and the ḥadīth, and disobedience cannot undermine one's affirmation of God and the Prophet. Despite disobedience not impacting one's assent, assent is strengthened or weakened based on one's conviction. If an individual merely believes in God due to the belief of their parents, while their assent is considered valid according to the majority of Ash'arī theologians, it is also considered weak. The preferred method of assent for theologians was therefore assent on the basis of reflection or rational proofs, or both, to the extent that some Ash'arī theologians such as al-Bāqillānī (d. 403/1013) and al-Juwaynī (d. 478/1085) went as far as to say that it is an obligation on each individual to know the proofs for their belief.[9] At the same time, these theologians had to accept that not every individual would be capable of knowing rational proofs for God, either because intellects vary or simply because individuals do not have access to scholars capable of teaching these proofs. For such people, then, their belief is contingent upon reflecting on the created world, which the Ash'arīs argued provides signs to lay individuals of a single creator. This argument of the created world as a sign of the creator returns to the Qur'ān itself, where God repeatedly states to the same effect: "it is He who spread out the earth, placed firm mountains and rivers on it, and made two of every kind of fruit; He draws the veil of night over the day. There truly are signs in this for people who reflect" (al-Ra'd [13]:3). Here things seem to come full circle: God has created the world so that He can be known and worshipped, and He has given humankind the ability to freely choose belief or disbelief, obedience or disobedience. For individuals who embark on the path of belief, the most basic belief according to the theologians is one that is arrived at through reflection upon creation. Creation therefore becomes not merely the disclosure of God in the world but also the proof of His existence.

God's Continuative Creation

Until now the discussion of creation has revolved around God's creation of the world, and more specifically what that reveals about God's nature and human obligation. But, given that human beings are created with choice, the implication is that human beings also have creative capacities to choose their actions. For theologians, this raised the question of what the relationship is between the creation of created beings and God's ultimate creative power. And perhaps most importantly, are the creative powers of either limited, and if so, how?

As noted earlier, each entity is defined by its unique ontology and abilities. For instance, what a tree is capable of doing differs from what a human being is capable of doing. Both the ontology and the capability of a thing are created by God. This is exemplified in the story of Abraham where he chastises his people for worshipping idols: "but [Abraham] said, 'How can you worship things you carve with your own hands, when it is God who has created you and all your handiwork?'" (al-Ṣāffāt [37]:95). In this verse Abraham argues that not only is God the creator of humankind but He is also creator of all actions of His creation. Elsewhere in the Qur'ān God commands Muhammad: "Say, 'I have no control over benefit or harm, even to myself, except as God may please: if I had knowledge of what is hidden, I would have abundant good things and no harm could touch me. I am no more than a bearer of warning and good news to those who believe'" (al-A'rāf [7]:188). And speaking more specifically to the continuous creation of human beings, God states, "We created man from an essence of clay, then We placed him as a drop of fluid in a safe place, then We developed that drop into a clinging form, and We developed that form into a lump of flesh, and We developed that lump into bones, and We clothed those bones with flesh, and later We developed him into other forms—glory be to God, the best of creators!" (al-Mu'minūn [23]:12–14).

When taken together, these verses present a paradox—God is the creator of the idols that distract one from worshipping the one true God, yet God is also the creator of human beings, whom He creates for the explicit purpose of worshipping Him. This raises the question, to what extent is God *creating* the idol and to what extent is the human? And if man is actively creating, does that mean God has another, more passive modality of creation?

These questions were particularly difficult for theologians to address because they had to uphold both the majestic creative powers of God and the ability of the human being to choose his or her own actions. If the latter was not preserved, then the notion of reward and punishment would be completely arbitrary as human beings theoretically should not be held accountable for any of their actions.[10] After being embroiled in extensive theological debates, the Ash'arī theologians articulated a theory of acquisition (*kasb*), arguing for both God's creation of human action and for human creation of action.[11] According to the *kasb* doctrine, once individual intention (*qaṣd*) for an action is solidified, God endows the individual, in the moment of their acting, with the power (*qudra*) to complete that action. Thus, it is the individual who intends to do the action and executes the action, making them responsible, but it is only through the power endowed by God that they are able to act. This implies that there are two modalities of creation—one in which God is actively creating, and one in which God is actively facilitating the creation of creation; however, in the Qur'ān there is also a third modality: actively managing creation.

The third modality, of God actively managing creation, comes forth in verses that describe God's active role in the world.[12] When speaking about inanimate creation, God states,

> It is God who raised up the heavens with no visible supports and then established Himself on the throne; He has subjected the sun and the moon each to pursue its course for an appointed time; He regulates all things, and makes the revelations clear so that you may be certain of meeting your Lord; it is He who spread out the earth, placed firm mountains and rivers on it, and made two of every kind of fruit; He draws the veil of night over the day. There truly are signs in this for people who reflect. There are, in the land, neighbouring plots, gardens of vineyards, cornfields, palm trees in clusters or otherwise, all watered with the same water, yet We make some of them taste better than others: there truly are signs in this for people who reason. (al-Raʿd [13]:2–4)

Notably, most of the verbs used to describe the actions of God are in the past tense, which supports the idea that God is passive observer of His creation.

Nevertheless, at one point the verse states, "He regulates all things" (*yudabbir al-amr*), using the present continuous tense. Prior to this statement, the Qur'ān uses past tense verbs to inform the reader that God raised heavens, mounted the throne, and compelled the sun and moon to be of service. Thus, while God *established* the elements to the celestial movement in the past, He *manages* the movement in the present. Similarly, according to al-Zumar (39):5, God "created the heavens and earth for a true purpose; He wraps the night around the day and the day around the night; He has subjected the sun and moon to run their courses for an appointed time; he is truly the Mighty, the Forgiving." This verse begins in the past tense when referring to what God created in the past but shifts to the present continuous tense when referring to God's continuous creative capacity in the alternating of night and day. The alteration between tenses is similarly used by the Qur'ān when describing childbirth:

> People, remember, if you doubt the Resurrection, that We created you from dust, then a drop of fluid, then a clinging form, then a lump of flesh, both shaped and unshaped: We mean to make our power clear to you. Whatever We choose We cause to remain in the womb for an appointed time, then We bring you forth as infants." (al-Ḥajj [22]:5)

The verse begins by explaining what God created but shifts tenses when describing the fetus in the womb and childbirth. In using the present tense, God indicates that He is managing the birth of the child whereas the process prior to, perhaps, the formation of a discernable fetus continues according to the nature of gestation. Elsewhere, the Qur'ān notes, "He is the One who originates creation and will do it again—this is even easier for Him" (al-Rūm [30]:27), once again using the present continuous, implying God is not only overseeing but is also actively involved in creating.

The oscillation between past and present tenses demonstrates the multiple modalities of creation: God has created and is creating. This dynamic is best summarized in the following Qur'ānic verses: "Your Lord is God who created the heavens and earth in six Days, then established Himself on the Throne, governing everything" (Yūnus [10]:3); and "God is the Creator of all things; He has charge of everything" (al-Zumar [39]:62). This does not mean that God is perpetually involved in the world, creating actions in each particular moment and overruling humankind's creative capacities; rather, God allows the universe and all that is within to function according to its nature, in the case of inanimate beings, and according to its intentions, in the case of humankind.

The three modes of God creating can be summarized as (1) ultimately creating, bringing both animate and inanimate beings into existence; (2) managing creation of inanimate beings and animate beings, which lack choice; and (3) facilitating the creation of creation. These three can be represented by the following verses, respectively: "He says only, 'Be,' and it is" (al-Baqara [2]:117b); "Your Lord is God who created the heavens and earth in six Days, then established

Himself on the Throne, governing everything" (Yūnus [10]:3); and "We guided him to the right path, whether he was grateful or not" (al-Insān [76]:3).

Reflecting on the theme of creation in the Qur'ān inevitably opens many avenues of inquiry. For theologians specifically, it raises a variety of issues ranging from belief to the relationship between God and human beings in relation to human actions. And although the Qur'ān clearly establishes the creative power of God, and the necessity of human reflection upon creation, the verses often pull scholars in a variety of directions, forcing them to recognize multiple modes of God's creative capacity. Irrespective of this, the Qur'ān uniformly implores individuals to reflect upon God's creation, as creation for theologians and exegetes alike is not simply a sign of God's majesty but the very signpost of His existence.

Notes

1. For an overview of early theological discussions revolving around the attributes of God and other themes, see John Renard, ed., *Islamic Theological Themes: A Primary Source Reader* (Oakland: University of California Press, 2014). One of the most important classical works of theology, Abu'l-Ma'ālī 'Abd al-Mālik al-Juwaynī's *Kitāb al-Irshād ilā qawāṭi' al-adilla fī uṣūl al-i'tiqād*, has been translated into the English language and can also be referenced to obtain a more advanced understanding of how these theological debates were interrelated. See Iman al-Haramayn al-Juwaynī, *A Guide to Conclusive Proofs for the Principles of Belief*, trans. Paul Walker (Reading, UK: Garnet Publishing, 2001).

2. The Mu'tazilite school of theology is a rational school of theology that flourished from the eighth through tenth centuries, primarily in Basra and Baghdad. Later the Ash'arī school came to dominate Sunnī Islam, with the Mu'tazilite school surviving only in piecemeal form subsumed within other schools. For an overview of the development of the school and its doctrines, see Josef Van Ess, *The Flowering of Muslim Theology* (Cambridge, MA: Harvard University Press, 2006); and Richard Martin and Mark Woodward, *Defenders of Reason in Islam: Mu'tazilism from Medieval School to Modern Symbol* (London: Oneworld, 1997).

3. In this essay, all quotations of the Qur'ān are from the translation by M. A. S. Abdel Haleem (Oxford: Oxford University Press, 2004).

4. The Ash'arī theological school eventually came to dominate Sunnī Islam. For its rise, relationship with other schools, and doctrine, see William Montgomery Watts, *The Formative Period of Islamic Thought* (Edinburgh: Edinburg University Press, 1973).

5. William Chittick, *The Sufi Path of Knowledge* (Albany: State University of New York Press, 1989), 391. Translation my own.

6. See Qur'ān 33:72a ("We offered the Trust to the heavens, the earth, and the mountains, yet they refused to undertake it and were afraid of it"). See also Qur'ān 55:6 ("the plants and the trees submit to his designs").

7. The paradigmatic example of a jinn disobeying God is the case of Iblis, who refused to prostrate to Adam after God's command. See Qur'ān 2:34, 7:12, 18:50.

8. Richard Frank, "Knowledge and *Taqlīd*: The Foundations of Religious Belief in Classical Asharism," *Journal of the American Oriental Society* 109, no. 1 (1989): 38–40.

9. Abū Bakr Muḥammad ibn Tayyib al-Bāqillānī, *Kitāb al-Tamhīd*, ed. Richard McCarthy (Beirut: al-Maktabah al-Sharqiyya, 1957); and Abu 'l-Maʿālī ʿAbd al-Mālik al-Juwaynī, *al-Shāmil fī Uṣūl al-dīn* (Alexandria, Egypt: ʿAlī Sāmī al-Nashshār, 1969).

10. Also see Qurʾān 2:281, 286; 14:51; 40:17; 74:38.

11. The theory of *kasb* was first introduced by Muʿtazilite theologian Ḍirār ibn ʿAmr (d. 200/814) and was eventually adopted by the Ashʿarīs with certain changes. Most importantly, whereas Ḍirār argued that God endows human beings with creative powers at birth, which an individual draws upon when engaged in any actions, the Ashʿarīs asserted that God gives human beings the power simultaneously with their desire to execute a certain action.

12. See Qurʾān 57:22–23, "No misfortune can happen, either in the earth or in yourselves, that was not set down in writing before We brought it into being—that is easy for God."

God's Creation and Its Goal

A Christian Perspective

RICHARD BAUCKHAM

THAT GOD CREATED "heaven and earth" or simply "all things" is a funda-mental Christian belief, repeatedly stated in scripture and featuring in the ecu-menical creeds. It entails an absolute difference between God and all that is not God—absolute in the sense that this difference is incomparable with any of the relative differences between creatures. The difference can be stated in a number of ways. For example, it means that all creatures are utterly dependent on God for their very existence as well as for being the creatures they are and for all that makes for their flourishing. This absolute dependence transcends all the relation-ships of dependence and interdependence among creatures and, so to speak, places them all in the same ontological category, to which only God does not belong. God is dependent on nothing other than God. Among other implications, this ontological discontinuity between God and creation entails a profound dif-ference between our knowledge of creatures and our knowledge of God.

Another way of characterizing the difference between God and creation is to say that God's existence alone is necessary (God cannot not be), whereas cre-ation's existence and the existence of every specific creature are contingent (they need not have been), existing only because God wills it. A statement that gets closer to the question of why God creates is that creation is entirely God's gift. Again, this implies a relationship between God the Giver and creation as God's gift that transcends all relationships of giving within creation, all of which are grounded in God's gift of everything. The distinctions between necessary and contingent existence and between divine Giver and created gift require that God creates in freedom. This undoubtedly implies that he acts under no external con-straint or influence, something that the Genesis 1 creation account expresses in the form of creation by God's sovereign decree. In what way God's freedom in creating relates to God's own character is a more difficult and debated issue, to which I briefly return later. Finally, another way of characterizing the difference between God and creation is to say that God is infinite and creatures are finite. In other words, creatures are by nature limited, especially by the fact that they can exist only in time and space. The traditional metaphysical attributes of God (omnipotent, omniscient, omnipresent, eternal, impassible, etc.) are simply ways of saying that God is not limited in the ways that creatures are.

At least since Thomas Aquinas, some theologians have said that the relationship between Creator and creation that I have just sketched does not in itself require that creation have a temporal beginning. An eternal world existing in absolute dependence on God would be a created world, distinguished from the Creator in all the ways I have described. Nevertheless, the Bible undoubtedly relates creation to a temporal beginning, and almost all Christian theologians have affirmed such a beginning, even if, like Aquinas, they have thought that the concept of creation does not itself require a beginning.

While the doctrine of Creation entails an absolute difference between God and creation, this does not preclude an essential sense in which creation resembles God. (In the case of humans, this is quite explicit in the biblical idea of humans as created "in the image of God," but other creatures also reflect God in a very wide variety of ways.) What God creates expresses who God is but expresses it in distinctively creaturely (and therefore limited) ways. The immense diversity of creation (which is undoubtedly even greater than we yet know) is related to the fact that any creature can resemble God only in specific and limited ways. Christian theologians have explored ways in which not only God's manifold goodness as such but also its Trinitarian form are reflected in the creation. That God creates by his own Word (John 1:1–2) encapsulates the idea that, in creating, God expresses who he is, while the Trinitarian self-relationship of God in himself is the ground in God for the relational character of creation, made up as it is of interdependent webs of relationships, and especially human relationships. Finally, it is important not to think of creaturely resemblances to God in isolation from God's active relationships with creation.

At least in the case of humans, this means that through knowing God and experiencing God's love, humans are drawn into ever-greater resemblance to God. From the kind of participation in God that creatures have through their created resemblances to God, creation progresses, in new creation, to participation in the very life of God.[1]

God's Presence to, with, and in Creation

In relation to his creation, God has often been said to be both transcendent (beyond creation) and immanent (present in creation). It is important that transcendence refers to difference (as described above) rather than distance. It is precisely because God is other than creation that God can be present to and in creation in ways that creatures cannot be present to or in each other. The presence of creatures to each other is necessarily mediated by time and space, but God, who is not limited by time or space, can be present immediately to creation. This is a key difference from Platonic or Gnostic approaches in which God cannot relate immediately to creation—or at least to this material creation—because God is so different from it. From a Christian perspective, one might say that such a God is *not different enough*. His difference is merely an extreme form of the differences that separate creatures from other creatures. Christian theology will maintain rather that God's transcendence does not impede but enables his immanence. At the same time, transcendence means that God is free to be present in creation or not, and that this presence does not exhaust God's being—that is, there is infinitely more to God than his relationship to creation.

The metaphysical attributes of God affirm that God is not limited as creatures are. In the tradition of "classical theism," they have been understood as excluding their opposites: God cannot be spatial, temporal, weak, passible, and so on. But this interpretation of them would seem to be itself a limit on God's freedom and is difficult to square with many of the claims of the Bible and the Christian tradition. But it is possible instead to interpret the metaphysical attributes as not excluding their opposites. God is not limited by space, as finite creatures are, but he is free also to be present in space. God is not limited by time, as creatures are, but he is free also to be present in time. He is free even to be weak and passible. In all such cases God remains transcendent beyond such creaturely limitations but can also enter the finite conditions of the life of his creatures in order to relate to them in various ways. The incarnation is a unique instance of this, a case in which God, while remaining God, exists also actually as a finite creature.

The doctrine of Creation itself requires a continuing and constant presence of God to creation in that it remains utterly dependent on God and can exist only as God sustains it in existence. But we should not limit God's immanence to this unvarying upholding of creation. In scripture and tradition, the providential and salvific activity of God require us to think in much more differentiated ways about God's presence and activity in the world. There are many different forms of God's presence: theophany, vision, encounter, word of address, conversation, inspiration, empowerment, providential care, sacrament, incarnation, and others. In these many ways, God's presence is not only universal (in creation) but also historical and particular. By adopting the interpretation of the metaphysical attributes suggested earlier, we can do more justice than much of the tradition has done to some of these forms of God's presence with and in his creatures. These forms of presence are ways in which God participates in the finite existence of his creatures in space and time and thereby enables them to participate in his infinite life. Thinking of differentiated forms of divine presence also means we can take seriously the kinds of divine *absence* that scripture describes.

More controversially perhaps, this line of approach will help us to envisage, in distinction from classical theism, ways in which God freely enters relationships with his creatures in which God not only affects them but is affected by them.

This has often been thought inconsistent with the kind of creator–creation relationship outlined earlier, but this need not be the case if we think of loving relationships that God freely undertakes. Of course, in view of the absolute difference between the creator and creation, we can speak only analogically (whether cautiously or adventurously) of what such relationships mean for God.

Continuing Creation

The account of the week of creation in Genesis 1 seems to differentiate rather sharply between God's creative activity "at the beginning" and his subsequent activity in the world. This is in line with the overall purpose of the primeval history in Genesis 1–11, which is to account for the world as we know it, subsequent to creation, the Fall, the deluge, and Babel, since this is to be the setting for the rest of the scriptural narrative. However, other biblical accounts of creation, notably those of Psalm 104 and Job 38, give a somewhat different impression in that there is no sharp break between what God does at the beginning and his active continuing role in sustaining and providing for creation.

In recent times the notion of "continuing creation" has been highlighted especially by attempts to integrate into the Christian doctrine of Creation what we now know about the long history of cosmic, geological, and biological development. It no longer looks as though the nonhuman creation was put in place at the beginning as a stage on which human history would then proceed. Human history so far has taken very little time indeed, compared with the eons of natural processes, and human history is so far occurring in only a tiny corner of the vast space of the universe. But the effect of modern knowledge has not only highlighted ongoing process and change in nature. It has also made it clear that creation in this sense of continuing creation occurs through natural processes of scientifically discoverable cause and effect. If the process is grounded in God's creative activity, then that divine activity involves creation itself in the ongoing work of creation. To show that this is not entirely out of tune with biblical ways of thinking, we might point out that, even in Genesis 1, not everything happens by sheer divine fiat. In two significant cases, God's command enables the sea and the earth to produce living creatures (Gen. 1:20, 24) while at the same time God can be said to have created these creatures (1:21, 25).

Some such discussions propose that we should therefore speak of creaturely cocreators with God. This is an especially popular move when human history is seen as continuous with evolution and human engagement with the nonhuman creation as a kind of taking charge of the evolutionary process. In my view, talk of humans as "cocreators" comes too close to the Enlightenment's tendency to see humans as gods set over the rest of creation, able to remodel it to their own designs. It takes us too far from our solidarity with all creatures as creatures of God and subverts the difference between creator and creation. In Christian form, it impedes the urgent task of recovering the sense of the human role in creation as a special role within creation, exercised in radical interdependence with other creatures, not a role that sets us apart from and over creation.

Creation out of Nothing (ex nihilo)?

Since the late second century Christian theologians have said that God created all things "out of nothing." This somewhat odd phrase, which arose from the encounter with Platonic and Stoic philosophies, is intended to deny that God created out of some kind of preexisting stuff, as a carpenter might make a table out of wood. "Nothing" should therefore not be hypostatized, as though it were some kind of substance or space or state of affairs. The phrase means simply that God did not create out of anything. There was no precondition for creation other than God himself.

Traditionally the Bible was interpreted as teaching precisely this. After all, if God created "all things" (as the Bible often says) how could there be anything out of which he created them? Paul says expressly that "God calls into existence the things that do not exist" (καλοῦντος τὰ μὴ ὄντα ὡς ὄντα) (Rom. 4:17). However, it is said that such language does not necessarily exclude preexisting material from which God created since no actual "things" would have existed prior to God's creating them, only undifferentiated stuff. It could be that biblical writers were unreflective about this issue, which only arose from intellectual engagement with Platonism by later Christian thinkers. Once it was raised and considered, "creation out of nothing" seemed to be the necessary expression of the biblical distinction between God the Creator and all other things, designated as his creation.

It is worth giving some attention here to the opening verses of Genesis since these have an obvious canonical importance as an account of creation and have also been the object of much modern debate, mostly as a result of comparison with other creation stories from the ancient Near East. For technical reasons the translation of verse 1 is debated. One option is to accept the traditional translation: "In the beginning when God created the heavens and the earth." On that view, which seems to me the more plausible, this statement is a sort of heading for the whole account that follows, forming an *inclusio* with the conclusion in 2:4a ("These are the generations of the heavens and the earth when they were created"). Alternatively, we could translate, "When God began to create the heavens and the earth . . ." But in either case it seems clear that verse 2 describes a state prior to God's first creative act, the creation of light: "The earth was an unproductive emptiness and darkness covered the face of the deep, and a breath of God hovered over the face of the waters."[2]

This does not describe a hostile force that God must conquer in order to create a habitable world. The kinds of ancient creation myths that depicted God's victory over chaos monsters or oceans are echoed in some places in the Old Testament, but there is no trace of them here. Nor are the elements of verse 2 (earth, waters, darkness) the stuff from which God then proceeds to make the world. Nor, finally, despite the dominance of this impression in the literature, does verse 2 describe a state of chaos from which God in creation produces order. The sense of the wonderful phrase *tohu-wabohu*, in the light of the use of these words elsewhere, is that the earth was unproductive: it could not produce or support life. From later verses we gather that it was submerged in the primeval ocean. The whole was enveloped in darkness, lacking the light that living things require. What God then does in the six days of creation is to create habitable contexts for living things to exist and thrive (beginning with light) and then to create the living creatures themselves. The whole of God's creative work is concerned with the creation of living creatures. The result is, indeed, an ordered world, but the order is the order necessary for living creatures of many diverse kinds to thrive. So the state of things in verse 2 is preliminary in the sense that it precedes God's work of creating a habitable and inhabited world of living things.

Although the existence of this preliminary state is not said to derive from God, it seems to me the text is at least open to being read in that way, especially as verse 2 describes the state of "the earth," which the summary heading in verse 1 says that God created. In a canonical context, these verses can be read beside the creation account in Proverbs 8, where Wisdom (the personified Wisdom of God) speaks of being brought forth "at the first, before the beginning of the earth" and "when there were no depths" (*t^ehomot*, cf. *t^ehom* in Gen. 1:2) (Prov. 8:23–24). Here, in a passage that seems to be a reading of Genesis 1, there is certainly reference to a time before the earth and the waters of Genesis 1:2 existed. Thus, it is not so clear as is often asserted that the Old Testament in its canonical form does not regard creation as an absolute beginning of all that is not God.

Creation out of Love

It is surely not possible to take seriously the biblical claim that "God is love" (1 John 4:16) without ascribing creation to God's love. The Bible does not explicitly do so. From the Old Testament we may gather that God created in order to take pleasure in creation, to "rejoice in his works" (Ps. 104:31). In Genesis 1, the refrain "God saw that it was good," repeated after each category of creatures appears, indicates God's approbation and appreciation of what he has created, while in Proverbs 8, at the end of Wisdom's account of her accompaniment of creation, we find her "rejoicing in [God's] inhabited world and delighting in the human race" (31). But the New Testament illuminates God's motives in creation further, though by implication rather than directly. It makes clear that God's activity to save and perfect the world is motivated by his love for it: "God so loved the world [here primarily humans] that he gave his only Son . . ." (John 3:16). If God so loved the world he had created, it must follow that he loved it from before creation and created it out of love. The New Testament passages that treat Jesus Christ as God's agent in the original creation as well as in the renewal of creation (salvation) are, among other things, indicating in this way the continuity of God's purpose of love for the world through creation and salvation.

To say that God created out of love is not incompatible with the freedom of God's decision to create. To say that God made a free decision to create is not to say that the decision was arbitrary. God decides and acts in accordance with his identity and character. More difficult is the question whether God's love in any sense needs to find fulfillment in loving relationship with what is not God. The position of classical theism is that God has no needs, and his love for creation is nothing other than benevolence that seeks creation's good. But scripture seems to portray God's love as more passionate and involved than mere benevolence, analogous to the kind of human love that is self-giving, vulnerable to disappointment and pain, but oriented to fulfillment through reciprocated love.

A Trinitarian approach to the issue may say that, because God is a loving relationship in himself, God does not need the love of creatures in order to be fulfilled in love and that the Trinitarian relationships of self-giving love are the ground for God's choice to go out of himself in love for what is not God. God's desire for creation is to share with creation the love that God is in himself. Although God does not need to create, by creating he can and does extend the circle of his love and find joy in bringing joy to his creation.

In contemporary theology there is a certain trend to speak of God's love as kenotic—that is, involving self-limitation on God's part. This is said to characterize God's love both in creating anything at all—since God must "withdraw" himself to "make space" for what is not God—and in giving creatures genuine freedom, thus limiting his own freedom to determine what happens to the created world. The latter seems to me more plausible than the former.

The Goal of Creation

Genesis 1 stresses the goodness of creation, but "good" need not mean "perfect." In Genesis 1, we might say God made a good beginning, creating temporal creatures whose good lay in movement toward greater participation in God's own perfection. But the disruption of the good creation by evil requires that God must redeem as well as perfect his creation. What we call salvation is a combination of redemption and fulfillment. It not only rescues creation from the damage done by evil but also completes the process of bringing creation to the goal intended from the beginning. The new creation is no mere return to the garden of Eden but the goal of the journey on which Adam and Eve had barely embarked before they were expelled from the garden.

There is both a correspondence and a difference between the first two chapters of the Bible and the last two (Rev. 21–22). In the beginning God creates all things;

in the end he makes all things new (Rev. 21:5). In the beginning humans live in harmony with all creatures in the garden; in the end they are reconciled with all creatures in a garden city, the New Jerusalem. In the beginning God gives mortal life (Adam and Eve could die, though the tree of life in the garden represents the possibility of not dying); in the end he gives the water of life and the nations eat of the trees of life (Rev. 21:6; 22:1–2), symbolizing creation's participation in the eternal life of God, beyond the reach of transience and death. In the garden of Eden God pays Adam and Eve an occasional visit; in the new creation he makes his home with humanity (Rev. 21:3), and humans, worshipping, look into his face (22:4).

These pictures of the goal of creation focus largely on humans—not too surprisingly, in a book written for humans. But the goal is explicitly the renewal of "all things," encompassing all creation. In Romans 8:19–23 we are afforded a glimpse of the solidarity of humans with other creatures. As they suffer our Fall, so they will share in our final liberation from evil and death. Modern ecological understanding of the world reveals how all creatures are connected with others in complex webs of interdependence. They cannot be themselves if abstracted from such relationships. The same applies also to humans. We are used to thinking of relationality as essential to being human, but this concept of relationality should include the indispensability of relationship to other creatures, which is too often neglected, as well as to other humans and to God. According to Genesis, only when God had created all creatures did he see creation as not just good but very good (Gen. 1:31), for the whole of creation is more than the sum of its parts. Correspondingly, only when all creatures participate intimately in the perfection of God's own life will the whole creation attain the fullness of creaturely perfection.

Additional Note: The Hebrew Verb *bara'*

The first three words of the Bible are *b^ereshit bara' 'elohim*, "In the beginning God created . . ." or "When God began to create. . . ." There is a remarkable feature of the word "create" (*bara'*) that theologians have not sufficiently considered: it is a verb that is used only with God as its subject. It occurs forty-eight times in the Hebrew Bible, and in no case here or in later Hebrew texts (eleven occurrences in Ben Sira, thirty-eight in the Dead Sea Scrolls) does it have any subject other than God. This is extraordinary. Does any other language have a verb that can be used only with God as its subject? Theologians are accustomed to think that all our language about God is analogical or metaphorical use of language that we also use of things in the world. Since God is not anything within the world but the transcendent other, this language cannot have, when applied to God, the same meaning as it has when applied to things in the world. Its use is justified because we suppose there is an analogy in God to what the language says about things in the world, but at the same time there is difference. God is not good or wise in the same way that creatures are good or wise; moreover, we cannot specify the difference. Our ordinary language about God always embodies at the same time both what we can and what we cannot know of God. It is all qualified by divine transcendence.

A word that is only used of God would seem to be very problematic. How can we know what it means? By translating *bara'* as "create" or by translating it by any English word at all, we avoid the problem. All possible translations of *bara'* are words that can also be used with creatures as the subject. But if we spoke only ancient Hebrew, how could we know what this word that is only used of God means? Probably it once had a wider use and came to be used only of God, but we know nothing of that wider use. It would be a long obsolete use that is unknown to the Hebrew Bible and not relevant to the meaning of *bara'* as it is used in the Hebrew language we know.

How can we know what *bara'* means? First, we can observe that it is sometimes used in parallel with other verbs, especially the two other verbs that are most commonly used in the Hebrew Bible to refer to God's activity of creating: *'asah*, a very common word for "to make" or "to do" (used 2,622 times in the Hebrew Bible), and *yatsar*, which means "to form" (used 63 times in the Hebrew Bible, 42 of these with God as subject). These words are not simply synonyms, but the use of *bara'* in parallel with them implies that it shares some overlap of meaning with them. It must have the sense of bringing something into being or bringing something about.

Then, second, we can look at what it is that God is said to *bara'*. The verb is used not only of God's activity in the beginning, as in Genesis 1, but also of acts in history. In this latter usage we find that what God brings about (*bara'*) are unprecedentedly new events (Num. 16:30; Isa. 41:20; 48:7; Jer. 31:22). For example, "I will do (*'asah*) marvels, such as have not been brought about (*bara'*) in all the earth or in any nation" (Exod. 34:10). Whereas *'asah* could have been used of any act of God, *bara'* is used there only because what God promises to do is something completely unheard of. The reference is to novelty such as only God creates. It is something that cannot come simply from the ordinary possibilities of the creaturely but only from the transcendent possibilities of God. The word *bara'* evidently points to what we can state only negatively about this kind of divine activity: that it does what cannot be done only with existing materials or conditions. I said "*only* with existing materials or conditions" because it is not always the case that *no* existing materials or conditions are involved at all. This was evidently not the case, for example, in God's creation of Israel, for which *bara'* is used (Isa. 43:1, 7, 15; Mal. 2:10). So we cannot say that the word *bara'* itself means "to create out of nothing" in the sense of the later notion of *creatio ex nihilo*. But it is surely significant that *bara'* is never used with an object or a prepositional phrase indicating material out of which God creates. In its use in the first Genesis creation narrative, it seems to come rather close to the meaning of the later technical expression "to create out of nothing."

The first Genesis creation narrative seems to use the two verbs *bara'* and *'asah* more or less interchangeably. They occur seven and eight times, respectively (*bara'*: 1:1, 21, 27 [*tris*]; 2:3, 4; *'asah*: 1:7, 16, 25, 26, 31; 2:2 [*bis*], 3), in the following pattern: ABBABBAAABBBABA. It is notable that *bara'* not only frames the whole account in the introductory and concluding statements but also, when used of individual acts of creation, begins and ends the acts of creation of living beings (1:21 and three times of the creation of humanity in 1:27). It seems clear that the very general word *'asah* is subordinated to the word that stresses the incomparability of God's creating. It is also notable that this first creation account, unlike the second in Genesis 2 (see 2:7, 19), avoids altogether the word *yatsar*, which is elsewhere quite commonly used of creation by God.[3] This is doubtless because *yatsar* conveys the image of forming with hands or fingers, a different image that would not sit easily alongside the image of speaking commands that dominates Genesis 1. It is often claimed that this creation account avoids *yatsar* as too anthropomorphic. Forming with hands is really no more anthropomorphic than speaking. But the image of speaking a command is used in this account in a way that transcends the human analogy: unlike human commands, God's commands themselves effect what they command. The same kind of disqualification of the analogy in the course of using it could probably not have been accomplished with *yatsar*.

Notes

1. See the section "Additional Note: The Hebrew Verb *bara'*," later in this essay.
2. My translation.
3. See, for instance, Ps. 33:15; 74:17; 94:9; 95:5; 104:26; 119:73; Isa. 45:18; Jer. 10:16; 33:2; 51:19; Amos 4:13; Zech. 12:1.

Appendix: Structural Analyses of the First Genesis Creation Account

Environments + Names	Inhabitants + Tasks
[Preliminary state: earth, waters, darkness: unproductive]	
Day 1: Light—separated from darkness God saw that it was good	**Day 4:** Heavenly lights Task: to separate day from night, to give light, to rule God saw that it was good
Day 2: Firmament—separates waters God names: Sky	**Day 5:** Water produces water creatures Birds in sky God saw that it was good God blesses Task: to be fruitful and fill
Day 3: Dry land—by gathering waters God names: Land and Sea God saw that it was good Land produces vegetation God saw that it was good	**Day 6:** Land produces land creatures God saw that it was good Humans in God's image God blesses Task: to be fruitful and fill and subdue Dominion over creatures of (5) and (6) All creatures of (5) and (6) to live from vegetation of (3) God saw all that he had made, and it was very good

Days 1–7	Created	Creation formula	*bara'*	*'asah*	Other Divine Actions
Intro: 1:1–2			*bara'*		
Day 1: 1:3–5	Light	God said, Let . . . And there was			divided named
Day 2: 1:6–8	Firmament	God said, Let . . . And it was so		*'asah*	divided named
Day 3: 1:9–13	Dry land	God said, Let . . . And it was so			named
	Vegetation	God said, Let . . . And it was so Earth brought forth			
Day 4: 1:14–19	Heavenly bodies	God said, Let . . . And it was so		*'asah*	set
Day 5: 1:20–23	Sea creatures + birds	God said, Let . . .	*bara'*		blessed
Day 6: 1:24–31	Land creatures	God said, Let . . . (Earth bring forth) And it was so		*'asah*	
	Humans	God said, Let . . .		*'asah*	
			bara'		
			bara'		
			bara'		blessed
					said, said
		And it was so		*'asah*	
Day 7: 2:1–3	Sabbath rest			*'asah*	finished
				'asah	rested blessed hallowed
			bara'	*'asah*	rested
Conclusion: 2:4a			*bara'*		

Scripture Dialogue 1

God's Creation and Its Goal

Passages from the Qur'ān

Al-Baqara (2):21, 29, 117[1]

[21]People, worship your Lord, who created you and those before you, so that you may be mindful [of Him] . . . .

[29]It was He who created all that is on the earth for you, then turned to the sky and made the seven heavens; it is He who has knowledge of all things. . . .

[117]He is the Originator of the heavens and the earth, and when He decrees something, He says only, "Be," and it is.

Āl ʿImrān (3):190–91

[190]There truly are signs in the creation of the heavens and earth, and in the alternation of night and day, for those with understanding, [191]who remember God standing, sitting, and lying down, who reflect on the creation of the heavens and earth: "Our Lord! You have not created all this without purpose—You are far above that!—so protect us from the torment of the Fire."

Al-Nisāʾ (4):1

People, be mindful of your Lord, who created you from a single soul, and from it created its mate, and from the pair of them spread countless men and women far and wide; be mindful of God, in whose name you make requests of one another. Beware of severing the ties of kinship: God is always watching over you.

Al-An'ām (6):101–2

[101]the Creator of the heavens and earth! How could He have children when He has no spouse, when He created all things, and has full knowledge of all things? [102]This is God, your Lord, there is no God but Him, the Creator of all things, so worship Him; He is in charge of everything.

Yūnus (10):3–6

[3]Your Lord is God who created the heavens and earth in six Days then established Himself on the Throne, governing everything; there is no one that can intercede with Him, unless He has first given permission: this is God your Lord so worship Him. How can you not take heed? [4]It is to Him you shall all return—that is a true promise from God. It was He who created [you] in the first place, and He will do so again, so that He may justly reward those who believe and do good deeds. But the disbelievers will have a drink of scalding water, and agonizing torment, because they persistently disbelieved. [5]It is He who made the sun a shining radiance and the moon a light, determining phases for it so that you might know the number of years and how to calculate time. God did not create all these without a true purpose; He explains His signs to those who understand. [6]In the succession of night and day, and in what God created in the heavens and the earth, there truly are signs for those who are aware of Him.

Hūd (11):7

It is He who created the heavens and the earth in six Days—His rule extends over the waters too—so as to test which of you does best. Yet [Prophet], if you say to them, "You will be resurrected after death, the disbelievers are sure to answer, 'This is clearly nothing but sorcery.'"

Al-Ra'd (13):2–4

[2]It is God who raised up the heavens with no visible supports and then established Himself on the throne; He has subjected the sun and the moon each to pursue its course for an appointed time; He regulates all things, and makes the revelations

clear so that you may be certain of meeting your Lord; ³it is He who spread out the earth, placed firm mountains and rivers on it, and made two of every kind of fruit; He draws the veil of night over the day. There truly are signs in this for people who reflect. ⁴There are, in the land, neighboring plots, gardens of vineyards, cornfields, palm trees in clusters or otherwise, all watered with the same water, yet We make some of them taste better than others: there truly are signs in this for people who reason.

Al-Ḥijr (15):26–31

²⁶We created man out of dried clay formed from dark mud—the jinn We created before, from the fire of scorching wind. ²⁸Your Lord said to the angels, "I will create a mortal out of dried clay, formed from dark mud. ²⁹When I have fashioned him and breathed My spirit into him, bow down before him," ³⁰and the angels all did so. ³¹But not Iblis: he refused to bow down like the others.

Al-Naḥl (16):3–8

³He created the heavens and earth for a true purpose, and He is far above whatever they join with Him! ⁴He created man from a drop of fluid, and yet man openly challenges Him. ⁵And livestock—He created them too. You derive warmth and other benefits from them: you get food from them; ⁶you find beauty in them when you bring them home to rest and when you drive them out to pasture. ⁷They carry your loads to lands you yourselves could not reach without great hardship—truly your Lord is kind and merciful—⁸horses, mules, and donkeys for you to ride and use for show, and other things you know nothing about.

Al-Anbiyā' (21):1, 16–17, 22–23, 30

¹Ever closer to people draws their reckoning, while they turn away, heedless. . . . ¹⁶We did not create the heavens and the earth and everything between them playfully. ¹⁷If We had wished for a pastime, We could have found it within Us—if We had wished for any such thing . . . .

²²If there had been in the heavens or earth any gods but Him, both heavens and earth would be in ruins: God, Lord of the Throne, is far above the things they say: ²³He cannot be called to account for anything He does, whereas they will be called to account . . . .

[30]Are the disbelievers not aware that the heavens and the earth used to be joined together and that We ripped them apart, that We made every living thing from water? Will they not believe?

Al-Ḥajj (22):1–2, 5, 17–18

[1]People, be mindful of your Lord, for the earthquake of the Last Hour will be a mighty thing: [2]on the Day you see it, every nursing mother will think no more of her baby, every pregnant female will miscarry, you will think people are drunk when they are not, so severe will be God's torment. . . . [5]People, [remember,] if you doubt the Resurrection, that We created you from dust, then a drop of fluid, then a clinging form, then a lump of flesh, both shaped and unshaped: We mean to make Our power clear to you. Whatever We choose We cause to remain in the womb for an appointed time, then We bring you forth as infants and then you grow and reach maturity. Some die young and some are left to live on to such an age that they forget all they once knew.

[17]You sometimes see the earth lifeless, yet when We send down water it stirs and swells and produces every kind of joyous growth . . . .[18]Do you not realize [Prophet] that everything in the heavens and earth submits to God: the sun, the moon, the stars, the mountains, the trees, and the animals? So do many human beings, though for many others punishment is well deserved. Anyone disgraced by God will have no one to honor him: God does whatever He will.

Al-Muʾminūn (23):12–14

[12]We created man from an essence of clay, [13]then We placed him as a drop of fluid in a safe place, [14]then We made that drop into a clinging form, and We made that form into a lump of flesh, and We made that lump into bones, and We clothed those bones with flesh, and later We made him into other forms—glory be to God, the best of creators!

Al-Rūm (30):20–25

[20]One of His signs is that He created you from dust and—lo and behold!—you became human and scattered far and wide. [21]Another of His signs is that He created spouses from among yourselves for you to live with in tranquility: He ordained love and kindness between you. There truly are signs in this for those who reflect. [22]Another of His signs is the creation of the heavens and earth, and the diversity of your languages and colors. There truly are signs in this for those

who know. [23]Among His signs are your sleep, by night and by day, and your seeking His bounty. There truly are signs in this for those who can hear. [24]Among His signs, too, are that He shows you the lightning that terrifies and inspires hope; that He sends water down from the sky to restore the earth to life after death. There truly are signs in this for those who use their reason. [25]Among His signs, too, is the fact that the heavens and the earth stand firm by His command. In the end, you will all emerge when He calls you from the earth.

Luqmān (31):10

He created the heavens without any visible support, and He placed firm mountains on the earth—in case it should shake under you—and He spread all kinds of animals around it. We sent down water from the sky, with which We made every kind of good plant grow on earth.

Al-Sajda (32):4

It is God who created the heavens and the earth and everything between them in six Days. Then He established Himself on the Throne. You [people] have no one but Him to protect you and no one to intercede for you, so why do you not take heed?

Al-Aḥzāb (33):72

We offered the Trust to the heavens, the earth, and the mountains, yet they refused to undertake it and were afraid of it; mankind undertook it—they have always been inept and foolish.

Al-Fāṭir (35):1

Praise be to God, Creator of the heavens and earth, who made angels messengers with two, three, four [pairs of] wings. He adds to creation as He will: God has power over everything.

Yā Sīn (36):36, 81–83

[36]Glory be to Him who created all the pairs of things that the earth produces, as well as themselves and other things they do not know about. . . .

[81]Is He who created the heavens and earth not able to create the likes of these people? Of course He is! He is the All Knowing Creator: [82]when He wills something to be, His way is to say, "Be"—and it is! [83]So glory be to Him in whose Hand lies control over all things. It is to Him that you will all be brought back.

Al-Zumar (39):5–6

[5]He created the heavens and earth for a true purpose; He wraps the night around the day and the day around the night; He has subjected the sun and moon to run their courses for an appointed time; He is truly the Mighty, the Forgiving. [6]He created you all from a single being, from which He made its mate; He gave you four kinds of livestock in pairs; He creates you in your mothers' wombs, in one stage after another, in threefold depths of darkness. Such is God, your Lord; He holds control, there is no god but Him. How can you turn away?

Al-Aḥqāf (46):3

It was for a true purpose and a specific term that We created heaven and earth and everything in between, yet those who deny the truth ignore the warning they have been given.

Al-Dhāriyāt (51):56

I created jinn and mankind only to worship Me.

Al-Najm (53):31

Everything in the heavens and earth belongs to God. He will repay those who do evil according to their deeds, and reward, with what is best, those who do good.

Al-Mulk (67):1–3

[1]Exalted is He who holds all control in His hands; who has power over all things; [2]who created death and life to test you [people] and reveal which of you does best—He is the Mighty, the Forgiving; [3]who created the seven heavens, one above the other. You will not see any flaw in what the Lord of Mercy creates. Look again! Can you see any flaw?

Al-Qiyāma (75):20–40

[20]Truly you [people] love this fleeting world [21]and neglect the life to come. [22]On that Day there will be radiant faces, [23]looking towards their Lord, [24]and on that Day there will be the sad and despairing faces [25]of those who realize that a great calamity is about to befall them. [26]Truly, when the soul reaches the collarbone; [27]when it is said, "Could any charm-healer save him now?"; [28]when he knows it is the final parting; [29]when his legs are brought together: [30]on that day he will be driven towards your Lord. [31]He neither believed nor prayed, [32]but denied the truth and turned away, [33]walking back to his people with a conceited swagger. [34]Closer and closer it comes to you. [35]Closer and closer still. [36]Does man think he will be left alone? [37]Was he not just a drop of spilt-out sperm, [38]which became a clinging form, which God shaped in due proportion, [39]fashioning from it the two sexes, male and female? [40]Does He who can do this not have the power to bring the dead back to life?

Al-Balad (90):4

We have created man for toil and trial.

Al-Shams (91):7–10

[7]By the soul and how He formed it [8]and inspired it [to know] its own rebellion and piety! [9]The one who purifies his soul succeeds [10]and the one who corrupts it fails.

Al-ʿAlaq (96):1–5

[1]Read! In the name of your Lord who created: [2]He created man from a clinging form. [3]Read! Your Lord is the Most Bountiful One [4]who taught by [means of] the pen, [5]who taught man what he did not know.

Passages from the Bible

Genesis 1:1–2:4

1 [1]In the beginning when God created the heavens and the earth, [2]the earth was a formless void and darkness covered the face of the deep, while a wind from God swept over the face of the waters. [3]Then God said, "Let there be light'"; and there was light. [4]And God saw that the light was good; and God separated the light from the darkness. [5]God called the light Day, and the darkness he called Night. And there was evening and there was morning, the first day. [6]And God said, "Let there be a dome in the midst of the waters, and let it separate the waters from the waters." [7]So God made the dome and separated the waters that were under the dome from the waters that were above the dome. And it was so. [8]God called the dome Sky. And there was evening and there was morning, the second day. [9]And God said, "Let the waters under the sky be gathered together into one place, and let the dry land appear." And it was so. [10]God called the dry land Earth, and the waters that were gathered together he called Seas. And God saw that it was good. [11]Then God said, "Let the earth put forth vegetation: plants yielding seed, and fruit trees of every kind on earth that bear fruit with the seed in it." And it was so. [12]The earth brought forth vegetation: plants yielding seed of every kind, and trees of every kind bearing fruit with the seed in it. And God saw that it was good. [13]And there was evening and there was morning, the third day. [14]And God said, "Let there be lights in the dome of the sky to separate the day from the night; and let them be for signs and for seasons and for days and years, [15]and let them be lights in the dome of the sky to give light upon the earth." And it was so. [16]God made the two great lights—the greater light to rule the day and the lesser light to rule the night—and the stars. [17]God set them in the dome of the sky to give light upon the earth, [18]to rule over the day and over the night, and to separate the light from the darkness. And God saw that it was good. [19]And there was evening and there was morning, the fourth day.

[20]And God said, "Let the waters bring forth swarms of living creatures, and let birds fly above the earth across the dome of the sky." [21]So God created the great sea monsters and every living creature that moves, of every kind, with which the waters swarm, and every winged bird of every kind. And God saw that it was good. [22]God blessed them, saying, "Be fruitful and multiply and fill the waters in the seas, and let birds multiply on the earth." [23]And there was evening and there was morning, the fifth day. [24]And God said, "Let the earth bring forth living creatures of every kind: cattle and creeping things and wild animals of the earth of every kind." And it was so. [25]God made the wild animals of the earth of every kind, and the cattle of every kind, and everything that creeps upon the ground of every kind. And God saw that it was good. [26]Then God said, "Let us make humankind in our image, according to our likeness; and let them have dominion over the fish of the sea, and over the birds of the air, and over the cattle, and over all the wild animals of the earth, and over every creeping thing that creeps upon the earth."

[27]So God created humankind in his image,
in the image of God he created them;
male and female he created them.

[28]God blessed them, and God said to them, "Be fruitful and multiply, and fill the earth and subdue it; and have dominion over the fish of the sea and over the birds

of the air and over every living thing that moves upon the earth." 29God said, "See, I have given you every plant yielding seed that is upon the face of all the earth, and every tree with seed in its fruit; you shall have them for food. 30And to every beast of the earth, and to every bird of the air, and to everything that creeps on the earth, everything that has the breath of life, I have given every green plant for food." And it was so. 31God saw everything that he had made, and indeed, it was very good. And there was evening and there was morning, the sixth day.

2 1Thus the heavens and the earth were finished, and all their multitude. 2And on the seventh day God finished the work that he had done, and he rested on the seventh day from all the work that he had done. 3So God blessed the seventh day and hallowed it, because on it God rested from all the work that he had done in creation. 4These are the generations of the heavens and the earth when they were created.

Psalm 104

1Bless the LORD, O my soul.
O LORD my God, you are very great.
You are clothed with honor and majesty,
2wrapped in light as with a garment.
You stretch out the heavens like a tent,
3you set the beams of your chambers on the waters,
you make the clouds your chariot,
you ride on the wings of the wind,
4you make the winds your messengers,
fire and flame your ministers.
5You set the earth on its foundations,
so that it shall never be shaken.
6You cover it with the deep as with a garment;
the waters stood above the mountains.
7At your rebuke they flee;
at the sound of your thunder they take to flight.
8They rose up to the mountains, ran down to the valleys
to the place that you appointed for them.
9You set a boundary that they may not pass,
so that they might not again cover the earth.
10You make springs gush forth in the valleys;
they flow between the hills,
11giving drink to every wild animal;
the wild asses quench their thirst.
12By the streams the birds of the air have their habitation;
they sing among the branches.

[13]From your lofty abode you water the mountains;
the earth is satisfied with the fruit of your work.
[14]You cause the grass to grow for the cattle,
and plants for people to use,
to bring forth food from the earth,
[15]and wine to gladden the human heart,
oil to make the face shine,
and bread to strengthen the human heart.
[16]The trees of the LORD are watered abundantly,
the cedars of Lebanon that he planted.
[17]In them the birds build their nests;
the stork has its home in the fir trees.
[18]The high mountains are for the wild goats;
the rocks are a refuge for the coneys.
[19]You have made the moon to mark the seasons;
the sun knows its time for setting.
[20]You make darkness, and it is night,
when all the animals of the forest come creeping out.
[21]The young lions roar for their prey,
seeking their food from God.
[22]When the sun rises,
they withdraw and lie down in their dens.
[23]People go out to their work
and to their labour until the evening.

[24]O LORD, how manifold are your works!
In wisdom you have made them all;
the earth is full of your creatures.
[25]Yonder is the sea, great and wide,
creeping things innumerable are there,
living things both small and great.
[26]There go the ships,
and Leviathan that you formed to sport in it.
[27]These all look to you
to give them their food in due season;
[28]when you give to them, they gather it up;
when you open your hand, they are filled with good things.
[29]When you hide your face, they are dismayed;
when you take away their breath, they die
and return to their dust.
[30]When you send forth your spirit, they are created;
and you renew the face of the ground.
[31]May the glory of the LORD endure forever;

may the LORD rejoice in his works—
³²who looks on the earth and it trembles,
who touches the mountains and they smoke.
³³I will sing to the LORD as long as I live;
I will sing praise to my God while I have being.
³⁴May my meditation be pleasing to him,
for I rejoice in the LORD.
³⁵Let sinners be consumed from the earth,
and let the wicked be no more.
Bless the LORD, O my soul.
Praise the LORD!

Isaiah 40:12–26

¹²Who has measured the waters in the hollow of his hand
and marked off the heavens with a span,
enclosed the dust of the earth in a measure,
and weighed the mountains in scales
and the hills in a balance?
¹³Who has directed the spirit of the LORD,
 or as his counselor has instructed him?
¹⁴Whom did he consult for his enlightenment,
and who taught him the path of justice?
Who taught him knowledge,
and showed him the way of understanding?
¹⁵Even the nations are like a drop from a bucket,
and are accounted as dust on the scales;
see, he takes up the isles like fine dust.
¹⁶Lebanon would not provide fuel enough,
nor are its animals enough for a burnt offering.
¹⁷All the nations are as nothing before him;
they are accounted by him as less than nothing and emptiness.

¹⁸To whom then will you liken God,
or what likeness compare with him?
¹⁹An idol?—A workman casts it,
and a goldsmith overlays it with gold,
and casts for it silver chains.
²⁰As a gift one chooses mulberry wood
—wood that will not rot—
then seeks out a skilled artisan
to set up an image that will not topple.

[21]Have you not known? Have you not heard?
Has it not been told you from the beginning?
Have you not understood from the foundations of the earth?
[22]It is he who sits above the circle of the earth,
and its inhabitants are like grasshoppers;
who stretches out the heavens like a curtain,
and spreads them like a tent to live in;
[23]who brings princes to naught,
and makes the rulers of the earth as nothing.

[24]Scarcely are they planted, scarcely sown,
scarcely has their stem taken root in the earth,
when he blows upon them, and they wither,
and the tempest carries them off like stubble.

[25]To whom then will you compare me,
or who is my equal? says the Holy One.

[26]Lift up your eyes on high and see:
Who created these?
He who brings out their host and numbers them,
calling them all by name;
because he is great in strength
mighty in power,
not one is missing.

Romans 8:18–23

[18]I consider that the sufferings of this present time are not worth comparing with the glory about to be revealed to us. [19]For the creation waits with eager longing for the revealing of the children of God; [20]for the creation was subjected to futility, not of its own will but by the will of the one who subjected it, in hope [21]that the creation itself will be set free from its bondage to decay and will obtain the freedom of the glory of the children of God. [22]We know that the whole creation has been groaning in labor pains until now; [23]and not only the creation, but we ourselves, who have the first fruits of the Spirit, groan inwardly while we wait for adoption, the redemption of our bodies.

Colossians 1:15–20

[15]He is the image of the invisible God,
the firstborn of all creation;

[16]for in him all things in heaven and on earth were created,
things visible and invisible,
whether thrones or dominions
or rulers or powers—
all things have been created through him and for him.
[17]He himself is before all things, and in him all things hold together.

[18]He is the head of the body, the church;
he is the beginning,
the firstborn from the dead,
so that he might come to have first place in everything.
[19]For in him all the fullness of God was pleased to dwell,

[20]and through him God was pleased to reconcile to himself all things,
whether on earth or in heaven,
by making peace through the blood of his cross.

Note

1. All Qur'ān passages in this dialogue are given according to the translation by M. A. S. Abdel Haleem (Oxford: Oxford University Press, 2004).

PART III

The Dignity and Task of Humankind within God's Creation

Creativity, Covenant, and Christ

Brandon Gallaher

"GOD IS WITH US" (Isa. 8:10). These comfortable words, that comfortable name, "Immanuel" (Matt. 1:23; Isa. 7:14) (Hebrew, "God is with us"), Jesus Christ, are words Christians cannot say without fear and trembling, without a hearty gratitude for God's awesome grace revealed in creation through Christ, who is the King before the ages and who has wrought salvation in the midst of the earth (Ps. 74:12). For in Christ, through Christ, and by Christ, in the Christian understanding, we have God, we know God, and we and all creation with us are lifted up, illumined, and become grateful sons of God by the Son of His glory. Creation and the covenant in Christ, which is the subject of this study, are the means by which Christians think together God's loving and transformative relationship with His creation and human action within it.

In offering a Christian perspective on the place of humanity within God's creation, I shall begin with the beginning of all things—with creation as a divine gift. From there, I shall turn to the issue of covenant and its relationship to creation. On this basis, we shall then consider the Christian understanding of the uniqueness of humanity and how this is expressed through humanity (man and woman) being created in the image of God. I will then speak to how this relates to Jesus, who is understood as the "image of the invisible God" (Col. 1:15); the one in whom all things were created and the mediator and reconciler of all things with God. I will argue that the image of God, from a Christian perspective, speaks to the mediatorial vocation of humanity. Mediation, I will contend, is humanity's participation in divine creation through harmonizing the divisions that exist in creation. This mediation has a vehicle: obedient praise or glorification of God with the offering up of the self as pure and willing sacrifice through a holy life. Humanity turned from this call in the Fall, but the belief is that in Jesus it is reattained and the Christian Church is called to be the embodiment of this call and gift insofar as Christians are called to be a "royal priesthood, a holy nation" (1 Pet. 2:9; cf. Exod. 19:6). This is not the vocation of slaves but of those who are the "children of God" (1 John 3:1). In praising God, humanity is believed to transfigure and sanctify the world. But this also implies care and right stewardship of creation. Humanity "works" the world so that its first fruits might be offered up to God in thankfulness. Furthermore, the human being is called to work their individual lives in the cultivation of virtue (Col. 3:12–17). The modern world, instead of caring for creation and obeying its Creator by living lives of holiness and gratitude, has turned toward creation in greedy consumption. The Christian perspective is that only through once more beginning to see creation as a theophany of God's glory and our lives as pure offerings of gratitude to God can we attune ourselves with the creative Word of God. In my effort here, I must be necessarily selective. I will draw on a variety of Christian traditions, but it will also reflect my own interests as a theologian. I am also, it should be said, presenting a theological ideal. Individual Christians and institutions have very rarely lived up to it.

Creation as a Divine Gift of Love

In speaking of creation as a divine gift, we must say that, if it is a gift, then it comes from a gift giver who gifts it from love. God, in the Christian understanding, did not simply awake one day and arbitrarily create the world. The world is not the action of caprice. God is a God who takes joy in Himself. This is sometimes expressed by Christian theologians by saying poetically that the divine hypostases or persons of the Trinity (Father, Son, and Holy Spirit)—with "hypostasis" in no way being understood as an "individual"—fully and completely pour out themselves to one another in love. This divine love, it is claimed, then bubbles up and spills, as it were, into the world in the act of creation. Meister Eckhart (c. 1260–1328) even goes so far as to identify the very love God has for Himself with His love for creatures:

> God loves Himself and His nature, His being and His Godhead. In the love in which God loves Himself, He loves all creatures, not as creatures but creatures as God. In the love in which God loves Himself, He loves all things.[1]

Another historical way of expressing this (sans the panentheism) is to say that in His life of eternal love, God had creation before Him in His mind. It is that reality through which He wished to express His love (as a theophany or appearance of God) and toward which He could express His love as an *other* to Himself. Maximus the Confessor (580–662) writes in this fashion:

God, full beyond all fullness, brought creatures into being not because He had need of anything, but so that they might participate in Him in proportion to their capacity and that He Himself might rejoice in His works (cf. Ps. 104:31), through seeing them joyful and ever filled to overflowing with His inexhaustible gifts.[2]

Creation and Covenant

According to Christian teaching, such a God who loves His creation everlastingly wishes to be bonded with it. It is for this reason that creation has often been understood as a covenant in Christian theology. By covenant I mean an agreement, a bond, even a contract, which God makes with all humanity, their descendants, and even every living creature (Noah) (Gen. 6:18; 9:9) or with his chosen people (Abraham, Moses) (Gen. 17:4; 34:27) through a chosen representative. The covenant is marked by a sign as a living memorial of the bond. In the case of Noah this was the rainbow (Gen. 9:12–17). In Abraham's case it was circumcision (Gen. 17:9–14), and with the Mosaic covenant the sign was the establishment of the Sabbath/Saturday as the holy day of rest (Exod. 31:12–17). In the covenant God promises He will be faithful. In the case of Noah this faithfulness was a faithfulness directed toward all creation. God promised that He would never destroy the earth by flood. In the case of Abraham this faithfulness was expressed in a promise. He promised He would make him a great nation and make his descendants as many as the stars in the sky and the sand on the seashore and would give them a land from the river of Egypt to the river Euphrates (the Promised Land). Moses in turn received a promise from God that He would make them His people, God's people, "a kingdom of priests and a holy nation" (Exod. 19:6; cf. 1 Pet. 2:9).

But a covenant, a sure bond established by God, requires a certain faithfulness and obedience in return on the part of humanity of God's chosen people. By tradition God gave Noah various commandants and laws he had to follow. In the case of Abraham the sign of the covenant (circumcision) was also the commandment that he and all his offspring were to keep from one generation to another. Moses was given the law found in the Torah (the first five books of the Hebrew Bible or Old Testament), which focused in and around the temple and the rites of sacrifice detailed in Leviticus. Jewish tradition says this was supplemented by the oral law (Mishnah), which we find collected with commentaries in the Talmud. Christians claim, and we see this detailed in the Epistle of the Hebrews, that the fulfillment, transformation, and renewal of the Old Covenant between Israel and Yahweh (i.e., the Mosaic covenant) is given in a New (eternal) Covenant that is sealed by the once for all sacrifice on the cross of Jesus Christ, who is understood as the incarnate divine Word. This sacrifice on the cross is understood to be for humanity's sins, which are envisioned as a "debt" owed to God because humanity has violated the law of God in Adam's disobedience in paradise. By the sacrifice of Christ, it is believed, the debt of sins of humanity is paid, the law is fulfilled, and humanity is reconciled with and sanctified by its Creator God. There is then a further theological move. Through human beings graciously having faith in Christ, who fulfilled the law and paid the debt, it is believed that they can share in Jesus's reconciliation with God and are then given a gift of communion and union with Him as "children of God" (Rom. 8:14–17; 1 John 3:1–2).

Now if this eternal New Covenant in Jesus is a once for all reality, and it is eternal, and even if the various covenants, notably the law, were but preparations, even foreshadowings of this true and great and Eternal Covenant, then some theologians have wished to go further and argue that creation, which was formed in Christ as the eternal Word of God (Col. 1:16), must be thought of us founded retroactively and retrospectively on this very New Covenant. So the covenant is not really "new" at all but ever ancient, ever new.[3] Creation exists, as John Calvin (1509–64) put it, as the "theatre of God's glory."[4] It was formed in anticipation of not only the Fall but also the reconciliation effected between God and humanity through the blood of the cross (Col. 1:20). Karl Barth (1886–1968) extends this idea further when he says that "God's glory is what he does in the world, but in order to do what he does, he must have this theatre, this place and realm—heaven and earth, creation, the creature, man himself."[5] Thus, creation, for Barth, is said to be in the will of God the "External Basis of the Covenant," but, more importantly in the divine decree, the "Covenant is the Internal Basis of Creation."[6] In other words, creation does not exist independently of God's reconciliation of humankind with Himself in Jesus as the Word of God, but it is spiritually instrumental by providing the means by which God might redeem fallen humanity: "Creation is the natural ground for redemption, and redemption is the spiritual ground of creation."[7]

Many Christian theologians would have difficulty with this position because they fear it risks conflating creation with covenant and giving the Fall as well as reconciliation with Christ a certain natural necessity. The Incarnation of the Son and Word of God, Jesus Christ, it is argued, is a consequence of the Fall and would not have occurred if Adam had not sinned. In contrast, there is another position that reflects a "minority report" of sorts in the Latin West that is sometimes referred to as "Scotist" (after Duns Scotus, c. 1266–1308) and can be seen in such key early thinkers in the Christian East as Irenaeus of Lyons (c. 130–c. 202) and Maximus the Confessor (580–662).[8] The teaching is that the Word of God would have become incarnate as Jesus Christ even if Adam had not sinned and no Fall had occurred. The ultimate aim of creation, such thinkers argue, is a personal union of God with His creation. However, there is an even further development of these ideas, controversial for many, as it wishes to think of the relations of the divine persons or hypostases of the Trinity as intrinsically kenotic. The cross itself, it is argued, was written into the foundation of creation as Christ is understood as the Lamb slain spiritually from the foundation of the world (Rev.

13:8).[9] The cross is the "watermark of divine love" imprinted on every creature and on nature as a whole, which only comes to light once the historical cross of the Word of God appears implanted in the midst of history and creation, thereby making "worldly being intelligible. . . to receive a foundation in their true transcendent ground."[10] But to understand the link between covenant and creation, we need to further explore the covenantal thinking I am detailing.

Covenant, Creation, and Divine Love

When the Old Testament speaks of the everlasting love of God (Ps. 103:17; Isa. 54:8; Jer. 31:3), it speaks of a love that is a longsuffering mercy and faithfulness directed toward His chosen people (Ezra 3:11) since it is a freely covenanted or bound "steadfast love" (Ps. 136): "I will make with you an everlasting covenant, my steadfast, sure love for David" (Isa. 55:3). Thus, the nature of the covenant defines and delineates the bounds of the love. In His love, God is free, and this is expressed by the fact that He is "Almighty" both electing or covenanting Himself historically with Noah and all humanity (Gen. 9:8–11), Abraham and His descendants (Gen. 12:1–4; 17:1ff.), and eternally creating and sustaining His creation (Job 40:2). Indeed, God is He who shall be what He shall be toward His chosen people (Exod. 3:14) in His mighty deeds, which they shall experience ("I am the Lord your God, who brought you out of the land of Egypt, to be your God: I am the Lord your God," Num. 15:41) since He is the one who forms light and creates darkness, makes for prosperity and creates calamity, does all things as all things are in His power. Thus, creation itself, in this interpretation of the Old Testament, is an expression of God's love, and that love is a love that binds itself to its creatures, promises itself infallibly to them.

In this perspective, it is God the Creator who initiates the covenant with or elects His chosen people ("I will make my covenant between me and you"; Gen. 17:2), not the people with God as they might make a covenant with the inhabitants of a particular land (Exod. 34:10–17; Jer. 31:31–33). He who made humanity can make them into a people. God, in the mystery of His ways, chooses or elects His people (Ezek. 20:5), not the people God (compare John 15:16). Thus, we may infer that He need not have chosen the people of Abraham, Isaac, and Jacob, just as He need not create the world but did so of His own good will like a man who picks "grapes in the wilderness" (Hosea 9:10). By choosing His people and by enacting mighty deeds in her midst, God makes known to the nations His power and glory (Num. 14:11–16, 21; Isa. 49:3ff.; and see Rom. 9:8ff.). God's people have their status by nature or birth and divine necessity, and they are obligated to freely acknowledge this fact (or not, and die). This initial choice of such a peculiar people ("the Lord set his love upon you and chose you"; Deut. 7:7), however, flies in the face of the fact that they were not a great people but small in number and were even despised.

Yet even in the Old Testament it is arguable that God can set His love upon someone who is not covenanted to Him as a part of His chosen people, such as Noah (Gen. 6:8–9), Job (Job 1:10), and, in another fashion, the resident alien or stranger and sojourner in the land of Israel (Exod. 22:21). Furthermore, as is noted later by Paul (Rom. 4), God decides to bless Abraham—it is said, due to His faith (and see Heb. 11:8–19)—prior to His covenant with Him (Exod. 12:1ff., 15, 17). In later Hebrew literature, such as the Book of Wisdom, one begins to see a clear universalistic determination for God's love moving from a restricted covenant with His chosen people to the saving love of God for all men insofar as God is not only "merciful to all" (Wisd. 11:23) but is said to "love all things that exist" (Wisd. 11:24) or "love the living" (11:26) since God's "immortal spirit is in all things" (Wisd. 12:1). And why should this be a surprise? For is not God the Creator of all humanity and not just of His chosen people? And does He not do both actions out of free love?

Christ, Creation, Love, and the New Covenant

God, the writers of the New Testament affirm, has set His love not only on a particular people but on His whole creation, but for these writers this is directly connected to Jesus Christ: "that the world may know that thou hast sent me and hast loved them even as thou hast loved me" (John 17:23). Once again, this love is a covenantal love, but now the meaning of the Old Covenant is said to be revealed as "Christ the power of God and the wisdom of God" (1 Cor. 1:24) or the one in whom there is now a gracious New Covenant of faith. Christ is made known as the "concise word" of the Gospel, which clearly sums up and fulfills the Law and the Prophets' call to God's people to "love the Lord your God with all your heart, and with all your soul, and with all your mind" and to "love your neighbor as yourself" (Matt. 22:37–39).[11] God, in this theological perspective, has bound Himself eternally to His creation in His eternal perfect "High Priest," Christ, the eternal Word of God, who "through the power of an indestructible life" (Heb. 7:16) serves as "guarantee" in this new "better covenant" (Heb. 7:22) of grace with His Body, the Church, understood to be the new "Israel" or chosen people (Gal. 4:26): "The Lord has sworn and will not change his mind, 'You are a priest forever according to the order of Melchizedek'" (Ps. 110:4; cf. Heb. 7:21).

Christ is understood in Christian teaching not only as the High Priest but as the "image of the invisible God" (Col. 1:15) showing forth the Father God (Heb. 1:3 and John 1:18). Human beings are said to be made in God's image and through this creation are called to be conformed to this image of the Son (Rom. 8:29). Indeed, it is said that Christ is, as the eternal creative Word of God, the one through whom all things and for whom all things have been created (Col. 1:16, John 1:1–3) as He is "before all things" (Col. 1:17). As the Messiah, the Son of David, He exists both before David (Mark 12:35–37, glossing Ps. 110:1) and

Abraham (John 8:53–59). Thus, as one of the rabbis put it, "The world was created . . . for the sake of the Messiah."[12] As the eternal Word of God, Jesus is understood to be the first in everything, in whom "all the fullness of God was pleased to dwell" and God "reconcile[s] to himself all things, whether on earth or in heaven, by making peace through the blood of his cross" (Col. 1:20). In this Christian theological perspective, creation and covenant come together in the Creator, Redeemer, and Word of God—Jesus Christ, the guarantor and living embodiment of the New Covenant.

So from a Christian perspective, creation and Christ, as the guarantor or surety of a better covenant, go together (Heb. 7:22). But if the New Covenant given to humanity with God in Christ is a free gift, it need not have been given, just as one will say that this is the case with creation, whose inner meaning is the covenant. Creation, so Christian teaching holds, need not have been created, just as the New Covenant in Jesus's blood need not have been made. God was free to create the world or not, and to covenant Himself with it or not. He is not necessitated. Creation is contingent. It is a free gift of love.[13]

Genesis: Creation and Covenant

In Genesis we can see how creation and covenant are thought together in this Christian theological vision. Humanity in the Genesis narrative is the last thing of creation that God forms. He forms creation for humanity, and humankind is given a special mediatorial role over creation through caring, overseeing ("dominion" [Gen. 1:26]), and tending to it as God's representative or viceregent (e.g., naming the animals [Gen. 2:19–20]). In this role he offers it back to God in thanksgiving. God gifts humanity paradise, which is envisioned as a garden he is called to continue to till and to keep and to live upon all its fruits if only he keeps God's commandment to not eat of the tree of the knowledge of good and evil (Gen. 2:15–17). Adam, prior to the Fall, as we can infer from the text of Genesis, had the possibility of knowing God in a direct way and engaging in some sort of dialogue with Him. Thus, we are told that Adam and Eve "heard the sound of the LORD God walking in the garden in the cool of the day" (Gen. 3:8).[14] Earlier we see that there is also union and communion between Adam and Eve as Eve is taken from Adam; they are one flesh and are naked and are not ashamed (Gen. 2:21–25). Moreover, there is communion, literally communication, between humanity and the animals as God brings the animals to the human being to be named (Gen. 2:19–20) and Adam and Eve, of course, speak with the serpent (Gen. 3:1–6).

That this state of being can be interpreted as covenantal can be seen both in the fact that, having created humanity on the sixth day as the pinnacle of the "very good" creation (Gen. 2:31), God rests on the seventh day (Gen. 2:1–3), which is a foreshadowing of the Sabbath of the Mosaic Covenant (Exod. 16:23–30;

20:8–11; 31:13–18; Lev. 23). Adam, as humanity, was indeed understood to be in a covenantal bond with his Creator explicitly by other parts of the Old Testament: "For I desire steadfast love and not sacrifice, the knowledge of God rather than burnt offerings. But at Adam they transgressed the covenant; there they dealt faithlessly with me" (Hosea 6:6–7). Furthermore, there is a sort of quasi-priestly or ministerial aspect to this vision of humanity as far as the "priestly" involves mediation; a reverent, grateful, and obedient attitude before God; keeping of His commandments; and care for His holy things. Indeed, the Hebrew terms used for tilling (*avad*) and keeping (*shâmar*) the garden in Genesis 2:15 correspond to the terms often used for explaining the Levites' duty to oversee proper worship at the Tabernacle/Temple (e.g., Lev. 18:5; Num. 3:7–8; 4:23–24, 26). The garden is like the Tabernacle (Exod. 40:34–38; Ezek. 43) in which the Lord God dwells and even walks among men (Gen. 3:8). Like the temple, paradise has an east-facing entrance, and, like the mercy seat of the Temple/Tabernacle, it is guarded by cherubim (Gen. 3:24; Ezek. 8:16; Exod. 25:22).[15] All that was required of humanity for God to remain faithful to bless them in paradise is that they keep the command of God, which is that they not eat of the tree of the knowledge of good and evil (Gen. 2:17). But to be in such a state of obedience is to live in a state of gratitude and thanksgiving.

The Image of God

The special covenantal bond between God and humanity (and with Him, creation) can be seen above all in the fact that humanity is said to be created in the image and likeness of God (Gen. 1:26–27). There is a long Christian tradition of theological interpretation of the *imago Dei*. As is well known, the concept, especially in Western Christianity, has often simply been identified with rationality or the mind, which is contrasted with the body. Thus, Augustine of Hippo (354–430), commenting on Genesis 1:26, writes, "From this we are to understand that man was made to the image of God in that part of his nature wherein he surpasses the brute beasts. This is, of course, his reason or mind or intelligence, or whatever we wish to call it." He then links this to Colossians 3:10, which speaks of the need for being renewed in the "spirit of your mind, and put on the new man, who is being renewed unto the knowledge of God, according to the image of his Creator" (echoing Eph. 4:23–24: "created according to the likeness of God"). Augustine concludes from this that humanity has been created in the image of God "not by any features of the body but by a perfection of the intelligible order, that is, the mind when illuminated."[16] It is perhaps due to this rational interpretation of the image of God that some in the Protestant West have argued that at the Fall the image of God is almost obliterated just as it becomes impossible to know God independently from divine revelation.[17] Another reason for this teaching of the near obliteration of the image of God may be the belief that at the Fall there is no longer any relationship with God possible on the human side without divine intervention, so no sure knowledge of God through that image can take place, so darkened it has become (Rom. 1:19–25). Whatever the case may be, this intellectualized exegesis is but one facet of a more complex exegesis in Christian tradition, and writers often add to the faculty of reason many other aspects, including personhood, creativity, and freedom.

A crucial exegetical issue concerns whether there is any distinction between "image" and "likeness" in Genesis 1:26. The rabbis make no distinction between image and likeness (which are treated as synonyms).[18] However, a distinction is made early on in Christian tradition, especially since Irenaeus of Lyons in the second century; his exegesis has had a profound influence on the theology of the Christian East or Eastern Orthodoxy in its different forms.[19] The Christian theological distinction of image (*tselem/eikon/imago*) and likeness (*demut/homoiōsis/ similitudo*) possibly originates from the fact that, in the ancient pre-Christian Greek translation of the Septuagint, or LXX (the Bible of the Jewish Diaspora and earliest Christians[20]), there is a "kai" (and, also) between the two words ("Let us make man according to our image and likeness" (Gen. 1:26 [LXX]), which was interpreted as a conjunction, whereas this is not the case in Hebrew ("Let us make man in our image, after our likeness").

Image and Likeness

For Irenaeus, Adam is created by Christ and for Christ in the initial position as body and soul animated by a breath of life from God's Spirit.[21] He understands "image," as in reference to the Son, as the image of the invisible God (Col. 1:15), whereas "likeness" he understands as in reference to the Spirit, who is referred to as God's "figure."[22] He says that the image of God is located indelibly in the flesh (i.e., the body) and the likeness is seen in the human soul animated by the Spirit. If the person lives toward God, in God's light, then his soul will manifest God's likeness in its breath animating the flesh, as a type of the Spirit.[23] However, if the person does not live toward God, then the soul's animating life is merely biological, and what remains is the flesh, which is a living corruptible body or body given life by a soul/breath that no longer points beyond itself but points instead to the grave.[24] Humankind, therefore, had the Spirit resting on it at the beginning.[25] The Spirit, Irenaeus teaches, vivified humanity bringing "true rationality [*veram rationem*]."[26] True rationality is to know without coercion that one should obey God and is the freedom to obey Him (life/good) or, out of ignorance, not to obey Him (death/evil).[27] Thus, the image of God might be understood as free, rational, and creative personhood with the innate possibility of partaking in conscious fellowship with God, and the "likeness of God" is an achieved reality when the image, by direct communion with the Person of the Word of God, Jesus Christ, through His spirit, is transformed into the finite image of the divine life.

But we need to return to the Christian connection of Christ with covenant and creation, for at the beginning, before it is claimed that humanity lost the likeness from the Spirit, humankind was said to be stamped for Christ according to His image. Humanity, the teaching holds, was foreordained for recreation or "a second creation by means of His passion which is that [creation] out of death."[28] Jesus Christ, as the eternal Word of God and Creator, not only precedes the created but He precedes the created precisely as its Savior, which means that the created is— not only at the end after the Fall but at the beginning prior to the Fall—understood as that which will be saved. In Irenaeus's words: "Since he pre-existed as one who saves, it was necessary that what might be saved also be created so that the one who saves might not be in vain."[29]

Image of God and Free Rational Creativity

The image and the likeness of God is, for Irenaeus, the almost godlike capacity to be self-determined and to mold one's life and surroundings, in this light either drawing close to God or rejecting Him.[30] Many in the subsequent Christian tradition will develop Irenaeus's idea, seeing the image and the likeness of God as free, rational, and personal creativity (*autexousia*). Therefore, to be made in the image and likeness of God is to have a free will or the power to act from within oneself such that one has power over oneself or is self-determining, *causa sui*. If one has such an internal capacity in the soul, then one can say that the actions that flow from such a free will depend upon oneself or are in our power.[31] Moreover, we must deliberate about those things that are in our power and can be done. However, such deliberation presupposes that we can choose between at least two possible acts (*a* or *b*) that are contingent, which is to say that we can just as well do *a* as we can do its opposite, *b*. Freedom, in this sense, therefore has a direct relation to rationality, for a rational being leads his nature rather than is led by it, as is the case with irrational beings. As Diadochos of Photiki (400–c. 486) puts it: "Free will is the power of a deiform [*logikes*, rational] soul to direct itself by deliberate choice toward whatever it decides."[32] This sort of freedom prima facie applies absolutely to God who, although He does not deliberate as this implies ignorance, is preeminently free or all-powerful (*pantexousios*[33]) because He has His Being completely from Himself (i.e., aseity) where will and nature are one. Human beings have a form of this freedom, but not absolutely. Besides being subject in their faculty of will to temporality and passion, human beings are always relative to others on whom they depend in their willing for certain choices and circumstances, so they must deliberate since their will is not their essence.

Humanity as Mediator

But in what does this free rational and personal creativity consist? At least one strong thread of Christian tradition says it consists of "mediation." By mediation I understand a process of unifying in harmony what is divided, but mediation also involves a sanctifying of creation through caring for it and stewarding its resources, a lifting up of creation to God in gratitude so that He may transform it, and an obedient trusting in God's law, which involves the self-cultivation of the virtues (Col. 3:12–15). The end of this mediatorial vocation is union and communion (as well as communication!) between God and humanity in creation as a created being called to participation in the divine life and to see God face to face in His glory (John 17:24; 1 Cor. 13:12). Humanity, in this perspective, is the pinnacle of creation standing between the spiritual realm and the material realm as belonging to both being an embodied rational soul made for spiritual union with God. This mediatorial role of humanity, involving humanity as a creature in between heaven and earth, called to gratitude and the vision and communion with God, is expressed nicely by Symeon the New Theologian (949–1022) in a poem in the form of a discussion between God and the author:

> And so I have said: by my power
> I blew a soul into you, (Genesis 2:7)
> a soul both logical and rational,
> which, as though entering a house,
> was united to your body
> and took it as an instrument,
> the one being appeared out of the two.
> I tell you a rational living being,
> a human who is double from two
> natures inexpressibly;
> from a visible body that is
> without senses and irrational,
> and from an invisible soul
> according to my image (Genesis 1:26–27)
> both logical and rational
> —strange marvel—amidst all things,
> between creatures, I say.
> Between what creatures?
> The material and the immaterial.
> For the material creatures are what you see,
> but the immaterial are angels.
> And so between these, I tell you,
> the double living creature, the human being,
> who is immaterial in perceptible creation,

but perceptible in immaterial creation.
And so I made him as perceptible
lord and master
of the visible creation,
setting all visible things
as servants under him alone (Psalm 8:6)
so that he would see my works
and glorify me the Creator.
And since he was rational
and contemplating rationally,
I granted that he see Me,
and by this I established him
in the dignity of the angels.
Look, understand what I say to you:
a human being, being double,
saw my creatures with
perceptible eyes,
but he saw the face of Me
the creator with rational eyes;
he contemplated my glory
and conversed with Me by the hour.
But when he transgressed
my command, when he ate from
the tree, he became blind
and entered into the darkness
of death, like I said.[34]

This middle position of humanity "a little lower than God" (Ps. 8:5; or following the LXX: "than the angels"; cf. Heb. 2:7) but above the animal kingdom gives
humankind the vocation of having "dominion" over creation (Ps. 8:6 and Gen.
1:28). He is as a sort of king of creation with "glory and honor" or, more properly,
viceregent as humanity is crowned by God (Ps. 8:5) and merely rules in God's
place. Part of this dominion is for humanity to procreate ("Be fruitful and multiply"; Gen. 1:28; 9:7) and thereby fill the earth, bringing order to creation. Yet to
"subdue" creation (Gen. 1:28) or to put all things under one's feet (Ps. 8:6) is not
simply to govern or order. It is also a matter of caring for creation, stewarding its
resources, and helping it to give up its bounty in a sustainable way. This all
comes under the idea of working the world and turning it into an orderly garden
reflecting the pattern that exists in heaven and in this way sanctifying it. But in
this perspective the vocation of humanity given by God is not only to transform
the world into an earthly paradise where all creatures may come to know and
praise their Creator (Ps. 148) through different species of ruling and working the
world; it is also to bring creation into harmony. It is here I want to expand on the

idea of "mediation" to further deepen the notion of human creativity within divine creation.

This is a major theme in the work of Maximus the Confessor. He holds that the cosmos, made up of visible and invisible things, is humanity as a macrocosm and conversely that "man made up of soul and body is a world" or microcosm.[35] Creation in paradise, though indeed "very good" (Gen. 1:31), still needed completion as it was still divided into extremes. Otherwise, why would God have asked humanity to till and keep it? The work of humanity in creation is not mere stewardship but a creative harmonization of the divine creation that was nascent and still capable of growing further into perfection from glory to glory (like humanity itself). These extremes in creation included the divisions of male and female, paradise and the whole world, heaven and earth, intelligible and sensible creation, and the whole of created nature *from* uncreated nature (i.e., the division of the world from God). Humanity was called "to draw all the extremes into unity" or "mediating through himself all the divided extremes" and in this way to achieve "the mode of their completion . . . and so bring to light the great mystery of the divine plan, realizing in God the union of the extremes which exist among beings, by harmoniously advancing in an ascending sequence from the proximate to the remote and from the inferior to the superior." Creation, according to Maximus, was called in paradise to union with its Creator, and humanity was to be the one in whom and through whom this union was to be achieved. Humanity had this capacity because it was "related to the divided extremes through his own parts." It is precisely because humanity can unite the extremes that it was created last as a "kind of natural bond mediating between the universal extremes through his parts."[36] And the unity to which it is bringing all things is to gather up all things to the Creator in a union of love where graciously the uncreated was united with the created, "the whole wholly pervading the whole God, and becoming everything that God is, without however identity in essence" as God is "absolutely unique."[37] This is the historic Christian teaching (found in both Christian East and West) of "divinization" or "deification" (*theosis*) or that humanity might become "participants of the divine nature" (2 Pet. 1:4).[38] But note the crucial proviso that this is by grace and in no way negates the enduring distinction between God and creation. Even if humanity participates in the divine life, it still remains created, and God still remains uncreated.

Mediation as Praise and Grateful Obedience to God

But how might this come to pass? Christian teaching holds that this process of unification or mediation to which humanity is called in creation as a free creaturely labor and whose end is union and communion between God and creation can happen only if humanity lives a life of gratitude, trust, and faithful obedience to God's commands. In being obedient to God, one must cultivate the virtues in oneself just as Adam cultivated his garden, thereby conforming oneself to the image in which one was created, that of the Son and Word of God (Rom. 8:29), so that one's image might be raised to the divine likeness. This is, quite simply, the acquisition of the Holy Spirit. Such a life was one where humankind lived toward God in lifting up the things of creation to Him in thankfulness as the pinnacle of the whole of creation acknowledging the God whose "eternal power and divine nature, invisible though they are, have been understood and seen through the things he has made" (Rom. 1:20). This is a God who is understood to be "clothed with honor and majesty, wrapped in light as with a garment" (Ps. 104:1–2). In this theological perspective, praising God as long as one lives and has being (Ps. 104:33) is to fulfill the law of God out of sheer gracious and faithful love, thereby drawing all creation toward the Creator in unity: "Let them praise the name of the Lord, for his name alone is exalted; his glory is above earth and heaven" (Ps. 148:13). But such an attitude is said to involve trust. It is a total reliance upon God like the ravens and the lilies of creation that are fed and clothed by their Creator (Luke 12:24, 27–28). It is to strive for the Kingdom, which is to ever be waiting on its Creator like the faithful slaves awaiting their master's return from the wedding banquet (Luke 12:35–38). In short, from a Christian theological perspective, humanity in paradise was called to sum up all things to God in a "sacrifice of praise" (Heb. 13:15) by presenting his body to God "as a living sacrifice, holy and acceptable to God, which is your spiritual worship" (Rom. 12:1). The ungrateful human being is the mortal man since both mortal and immortal life are from God, but immortality is the special gift of the Spirit of God to the human being with a grateful heart.

The Creative Humility of Adam

Adam was called to cultivate the garden in Eden that God planted for him (Gen. 2:8, 15). This consisted both of unifying creation in himself, which we can see in his naming of the animals (Gen. 2:19–20), but he did this precisely through referring all of that creation, including himself as its head, back to God. He lifted it up beyond itself and himself to its source and origin, naming and claiming it as his own and, in giving it his own stamp or name, appropriating it for its Creator, God. But this elevation of creation required both gratitude for the gift of life given to humankind seen in the tree of life upon which they fed and which gave him immortality (Gen. 2:9; 3:22, 24) and above all a rich receptiveness or trust in all of God's commands—that is, a humility or groundedness of heart (Latin, *humilis* [humble] being related to *humus* [earth, soil]). Such creative humility of Adam would have allowed him to accept the apparently arbitrary command of not eating of the Tree of the Knowledge of Good and Evil (Gen. 2:16–17). Creation and humanity were mortal, and both could live only through humankind's constant referral of the gifts of the world and himself back to God, by his offering of it as mediator or "priest of creation" to his Creator.[39]

Putting this Christian theological perspective slightly differently, the initial vocation of humanity, as summit, summary, king, and microcosm of creation, is for him to consciously, freely, and thankfully appropriate the world and his own nature given to him as a good gift from the Creator and in this way making it both his own and God's own, good for himself and all creation in finding its union with God. When humanity offers up itself and creation to God, it then receives it back transformed into a new humanity and new creation partaking of the divine life, the Spirit, graciously synthesizing in itself the uncreated with the created. In other words, by freely making his own what is gifted to him by God, humanity starts the process of transforming the divine imprint—the image of God—more and more into the likeness of God so that he might have a "share of [the very same] being"[40] that is the divine life, becoming a participant of the divine nature (2 Pet. 1:4). This led Maximus the Confessor and Gregory of Nazianzus (c. 329–90) audaciously to call humanity a "portion of God."[41] Thus, the vocation of humanity, according to this Christian perspective, is to be a mediator in creating, accepting, and transforming creation into the divine life of love of God and with it becoming adopted sons and daughters of God "through grace by imitation."[42] This in *no way* makes a human being a "god" by substance, for the creature *is not and never will be* its Creator. That would be pantheism, polytheism, and idolatry from a Christian perspective. Indeed, it is precisely because of these reservations that some Protestants reject the teaching of deification, though it is held in different forms by the Roman Catholic and Orthodox churches. It is argued that when humanity makes the divine life his own, when he takes it with gratitude into himself, he then can turn to creation and renew the face of the earth and sanctify it. But this calling of mediation as a free creative praise leading to union of the uncreated and the created was never attained by humanity.[43]

The Fall and the Loss of Humanity's Vocation as Mediator / Priest of Creation

From a Christian perspective, when human beings disobeyed God, they condemned the world and themselves to death and took it from its calling to be united with God through Himself as mediator. In the death of humanity, the world and humankind itself were tipped back into the ground from which they came. Now begins a process of de-creation, or falling back into the nothingness from which creation came. This state of living death is an existence outside the presence of God and His Holy Word (Matt. 4:4), which brings life eternal. Humanity, it is argued, turned from its vocation of mediation and fell by freely giving in to temptation by Satan. Instead of consciously accepting its own nature as a good and divinizing gift from the hands of God, it instead turned to the world and fed on it, greedily and resentfully partaking of it as if its life depended entirely upon it. In this way, humanity became a slave to both his own nature and his surroundings so that he no longer lived through contemplation and communication with God. In the Fall, the human being deluded himself that this participation in the world was his lordship over it and even his liberation from dependence on God such that he went from being a son of God by divine adoption to a self-raised God by auto-divinization (Gen. 3:4, 22). Such blindness to reality, existing in a darkness of nonexistence as true life is to exist by having one's sustenance from the hands of God, ultimately leads, Christian teaching holds, to intense misery, suffering, and finally physical death.

In Genesis, Adam and Eve, having disobeyed and knowing this in shame, hide themselves in the trees from God (Gen. 3:8), thereby blocking off encounter between God and themselves. It is as if they go from a state where they stand out from the rest of nature as its crown and summary to a reduction back to the very elements from which they were made. They are alienated from God, from themselves, and from the higher mission of freedom and creativity to which they were called in being formed in the image and likeness of God and asked to obediently follow the law of God. That this is not the normal state of affairs can be seen in God's reaction. He asks them after the Fall when they are hiding from Him, "Where are you?" (Gen. 3:9). They now are conscious of their break with God, their falling away from their true vocation, and Adam answers that when he heard God walking, he was fearful "because I was naked" and hid himself (Gen. 3:10). Once they eat of the fruit, the text says their eyes were opened and knew they were naked and out of shame sewed fig leaves together into aprons to hide their nakedness (Gen. 3:7).

In this passage, we see willful miscommunication between God and humanity on the human being's part. Adam hides himself from God so he *can't communicate*, and God immediately divines that the basis of their covenant is broken, for He says, "Who told you that you were naked? Have you eaten from the tree of which I commanded you not to eat?" (Gen. 3:11). But this radical fissure, this lack of communicative reciprocity now spreads into all the relationships in creation, and Adam immediately blames Eve (Gen. 3:12). But in blaming her, he tacitly blames God Himself, as he says that the person responsible was "the woman whom you gave to be with me" as if it is God's fault in some sense for having given him someone as a helpmate who led him astray. When God asks Eve, she then blames the serpent (Gen. 3:13) for having deceived her. It is then that we see, with the cursing of the serpent, the beginning of our present order with the animals at odds with both their Creator and with the one whom was their crown, head, and leader upward toward God—that is, humanity (Gen. 3:14–15).

There is in this Christian theological picture no communication, no free intercourse and creativity, no gratitude, and no obedience and striving for perfection and harmony. There is, in short, no mediation and no communion and union with God. Humanity is no longer the priest of creation. All that exists is sorrow, with women being cursed by finding their primary place as brood mares producing children in agony and having their husbands rule over them where presumably there was previously a free equality between the sexes, and now there is only an obligation (laying heaviest on women) to continue the human race (Gen. 3:16). Humanity is also cut off from God and from nature as he is no longer allowed to remain in the garden, which he previously tended to harmoniously and in serenity. The earth itself now becomes a curse to Adam, as he must suffer working it (with its thorns and thistles) to survive until he returns to it at death as dust to dust (Gen. 3:17–19).

Having broken their covenant with God, humanity is driven out of paradise (Gen. 3:24), out of a state of communion and union with God, themselves, and the rest of creation. God even has an angel at the entrance who now guards humankind from slipping back in and eating of the tree of life. With the advent of death, God thereby prevents humanity existing in an eternal state of alienation. God, many Christian teachers have claimed, has compassion on humanity and does not want this state of brokenness to continue to exist forever as man's physical death ends it. But there also is the sense here that God, in putting an angel to guard paradise, which was the state of free communion with humanity and free creativity, has permanently acknowledged a break with humanity that only He now can mend. Only He can bring back humanity to paradise and remove the blockage that prevents communion between Him and humankind—that is, the cherubim with the flaming sword (Gen. 3:24). Later the New Testament will describe fallen humanity (man unreconciled to God) as being a slave to sin (Rom. 6:6, 16–23), in "bondage to decay" (Rom. 8:21); and even as an enemy of God (Rom. 5:10) (though it does not say God is our enemy).

Reattaining the Vocation of Mediation / Priest of Creation in Christ as the High Priest of Salvation

Yet Christian teaching holds that this was not the end of the road, for God does not give up on His creation, the work of His hands. God is not willing that creation should lead a life of eternal death. He mercifully put an end to humanity's eternal life of death in physical death and turned them out of paradise into the world. In His mercy, it is said that God continually drew His creation back to its initial vocation to unite heaven and earth in itself through His covenants, culminating in the New Covenant sealed by God Himself, as the New or Second Adam, the eternal Word, Jesus Christ. God calls creation to live out in the world the "image of Christ" in which they were formed.[44] In Christ, the path of mediation and of an obedient, gratitude-filled harmonization of creation with God is opened up once again. Having lost in the Fall the mediatorial calling or the priestly garment, humanity/Adam as priest of creation is said to gain it back in Jesus Christ/the Second Adam understood as the eternal "high priest" of salvation (Heb. 3:1; 4:14; 5:8–10; 7:26ff.).[45] Christian teaching holds that in Christ, as the Second Adam *and* eternal Word of God, humanity has not merely a creaturely means to partaking of the divine life (as was the case with the first Adam) but also a divine means. Christ calls humanity in His "Body" the Church (1 Cor. 12:27) to a life of grateful obedience—becoming a "royal priesthood, a holy nation" (1 Pet. 2:9; cf. Exod. 19:6)—lifting up creation on high and caring for it as a gift of love from its Creator. This vocation and ideal is also expressed in terms of adoption as sons (Eph. 1:5) or becoming "children of God" (1 John 3:1; Rom. 8:16). Here the way of egotism is to be put aside, and it is hoped that through the communal work of the Church, there is begun the process of re-achieving in Christ the vocation of mediation. The members of the Church are called as Adam was called before them to work with God as cocreators through obedient and loving praise, thereby uniting what is divided and bringing creation into harmony. Sadly, as can be seen from a quick scan of Christian history and contemporary events, this high vocation and ideal has rarely been taken up by Christians, who most of the time follow the old Adam in living lawless, ungrateful, and disobedient lives in rebellion from their Creator. But such, at least, is the Christian ideal, as some in the tradition have understood it.

A Vision Still Relevant?

But is this Christian vision of creation as grateful and obedient mediation of divisions, as priests of creation, still relevant in a secular world? Even if we do not accept Maximus's idea of the fivefold division in the cosmos, the world is indeed lacerated by self-inflicted wounds such as an economic system built on the systematic plundering of the earth's resources that is so unjust that less than 1 percent of the population own more wealth than the other 99 percent and "Christian nations" claiming a righteousness from heaven while they wage war against their enemies through television and satellites thousands of miles away. Perhaps a new reappropriation of this ancient Christian vision of divine creation as a theophany of divine love and human participation in that creation as a grateful and obedient priestly mediation may lead a few steps closer toward harmony in this fragmented world.

Notes

1. Meister Eckhart, Sermon 56, *The Complete Mystical Works of Meister Eckhart*, trans. Maurice O'C. Walshe (New York: Crossroad, 1991), 293.

2. Maximus the Confessor, *400 Chapters on Love*, 3.46 *Patrologia Graeca* [PG] 90, 1029C in *The Philokalia*, trans. G. Palmer, Philip Sherrard, Kallistos Ware, vol. 2 (London: Faber & Faber, 1981), 90.

3. Augustine of Hippo, *Confessions*, trans. Henry Chadwick (Oxford: Oxford University Press, 1998), 10.27.38.

4. John Calvin, *Concerning the Eternal Predestination of God*, trans. J. Reid (Louisville: Westminster John Knox), 97.

5. Karl Barth, "A Theological Dialogue," *Theology Today* 19, no. 2 (July 1962): 171–77 at 172.

6. Karl Barth, *Church Dogmatics*, vol. 3, *The Doctrine of Creation*, ed. T. F. Torrance and G. W. Bromiley (Edinburgh: T&T Clark, 1958), part 1, 94ff. and 228ff.

7. Barth, "Theological Dialogue," 172.

8. See Allan B. Wolter, "Duns Scotus on the Predestination of Christ," *The Cord: A Franciscan Spiritual Review* 5 (December 1955): 366–72; Juniper B. Carol, *Why Jesus Christ: Thomistic, Scotistic and Conciliatory Perspectives* (Manassas, VA: Trinity Communications, 1986), 120–479; Daniel P. Horan, "How Original Was Scotus on the Incarnation? Reconsidering the History of the Absolute Predestination of Christ in Light of Robert Grosseteste," in *Heythrop Journal* 53, no. 3 (May 2011): 374–91; Irenaeus of Lyons, *Adversus omnes Haereses [AH]/Contre les Hérésies, Sources chrétiennes [SC]*, trans. and ed. Adelin Rousseau et al. (Paris: Cerf, 1965–82), 3.22.3; and Maximus the Confessor, *Ad Thalassium* 22 (*CCSG* 7:137–43) and 60 (*CCSG* 22:73–81) in *On the Cosmic Mystery of Christ: Selected Writings from Maximus the Confessor*, trans. Paul M. Blowers and Robert Louis Wilken (Crestwood, NY: St. Vladimir's Seminary Press, 2003), 115–18, 123–29.

9. On the cross written into creation, cf. Justin Martyr, *Iustini martyris apologiae pro christianis*, ed., M. Marcovich, *Patristische Texte und Studien [PTS]* 38 (Berlin/NY: De Gruyter, 1994), *1. Apol.* 60, 116–17 (citing Plato, *Timaeus*, 36b); Irenaeus of Lyons, *AH* 5.18.3, *SC* 153: pp. 244–45 [Armenian fragment]; and Irenaeus of Lyons, *On the Apostolic Preaching [Dem.]*, trans. John Behr (Crestwood, NY: St. Vladimir's Seminary Press, 1997), §34. For Christ as "the Lamb slain from the foundation of the world" (Rev. 13:8), see Sergii Bulgakov, *The Lamb of God*, abr., trans. and ed. Boris Jakim (Grand Rapids, MI: Eerdmans, 2008); Jürgen Moltmann, *The Trinity and the Kingdom*, trans. Margaret Kohl (Minneapolis: Fortress Press, 1993 [1980]); and Hans Urs von Balthasar, *Mysterium Paschale*, trans. Aidan Nichols (San Francisco: Ignatius Press, 2000).

10. Hans Urs von Balthasar, *Love Alone Is Credible*, trans. D. C. Schindler (San Francisco: Ignatius Press, 2004), 142. Here a comment of Martin Bieler is apposite, echoing Balthasar: "creation is ordered to man and his concrete history, this history, within divine Providence, casts its shadows on all of creation, which exists in solidarity with man. The Cross and the Resurrection are from the very beginning the watermark the Creator has imprinted on creation, but he has done so in order to make everything finally serve the fulfillment that comes with the revelation of the freedom of the glory of God's children." Martin Bieler, "Creation, Evolution, and the Drama of Redemption," *Communio* 33, no. 2 (Summer 2006): 305–9 at 308.

11. "Concise word": Irenaeus of Lyons, *Dem.*, §87, p. 93.

12. *Sanhedrin* 98b, trans. Joseph Shachter and H. Freedman, ed. Isidore Epstein (London: Soncino Press, 1936), 668; See this text cited in Benedict XVI, "General Audience Address of 7 September 2005," Libreria Editrice Vaticana, http://w2.vatican.va/content/benedict-xvi/en/audiences/2005/documents/hf_ben-xvi_aud_20050907.html.

13. For further discussion, see Brandon Gallaher, *Freedom and Necessity in Modern Trinitarian Theology* (Oxford: Oxford University Press, 2016).

14. Irenaeus of Lyons (*Dem.* 12) and Theophilus of Antioch (*To Autolycus* 2.22) interpret this passage in reference to the Son or Logos walking and talking to Adam in the garden prefiguring the coming of Christ who dwells among men. Theophanies of God were often interpreted in early Patristic writers as being of the Logos or Son of God

(Irenaeus, *Dem.* 44–45) as "the Father is the invisible of the Son, but the Son is the visible of the Father" (*AH* 4.6.6).

15. See Gordon Wenham, *Genesis 1–15* (Nashville: Thomas Nelson, 1987), 67, 87, and 90.

16. Augustine of Hippo, *The Literal Meaning of Genesis*, vol. 1, 3.20.30, trans. John Hammond Taylor, Ancient Christian Writers no. 41 (New York: Paulist Press, 1982), 96.

17. See John Calvin, *Institutes of the Christian Religion*, 2 vol., trans. Ford Lewis Battles, ed. John McNeill (Philadelphia: Westminster, 1960), 1:1.15.3–4, 186–90, and 1:3.7.6, 696–97.

18. See *Genesis Rabbah: The Judaic Commentary to the Book of Genesis: A New American Translation*, vol. 1: *Parashiyyot One through Thirty-Three on Genesis 1:1 to 8:14*, trans. and ed. Jacob Neusner (Atlanta: Scholars Press, 1985), Parashah Eight, 10–11, and Genesis 1:26.

19. See Irenaeus of Lyons, *AH* 5.6.1 and 5.16.1–2.

20. See T. M. Law, *When God Spoke Greek: The Septuagint and the Making of the Christian Bible* (New York: Oxford University Press, 2013).

21. Irenaeus of Lyons, *AH* 5.1.3 and 12.1.

22. On "image": Irenaeus of Lyons, *Dem.* 22; and Irenaeus of Lyons, *AH* 5.16.2; and cf. 2 Cor. 4:4. On "likeness": *figuratio* (*AH* 4.7.4). *Ante-Nicene Fathers* translates as *similitude*; cf. ibid., 5.6.1.

23. Ibid., 3.24.1.

24. Ibid., 5.6.1.

25. Ibid., 4.33.15.

26. Ibid., 4.4.3.

27. Irenaeus of Lyons, *Dem.* 11, *AH* 4.4.3 and 37.1–5.

28. Ibid., 5.23.2.

29. "Cum enim praeexsisteret saluans, oportebat et quod saluaretur fieri, uti non vacuum sit saluans" (ibid., 3.22.3 (*SC* 211: pp. 438–39); Cf. Martin Luther: "He created us for this very purpose, to redeem and sanctify us." Martin Luther, *Large Catechism*, 64, *Book of Concord* (Philadelphia: Fortress, 1959), 419.

30. See Basil of Caesarea, "Homily on Psalm 48," 8, *Exegetic Homilies*, trans. Agnes Way, *The Fathers of the Church*, 46 (Washington, DC: Catholic University of America Press, 1963), 324–25 [*PG* 29b.449B–C]; and Maximus the Confessor, *The Disputation with Pyrrhus*, trans. Joseph Farrell (South Canaan, PA: St. Tikhon's Seminary Press, 1990), 25 [*Disput s Pirrom*, ed. and trans. D. Pospelov (Moscow: Khram Sofii Premudrosti Bozhiei, 2004), 304C–D, 170–71]; and commentary at William Telfer, "Autexousia," *Journal of Theological Studies* 8, no. 1 (1957): 123–28.

31. John of Damascus, *St. John of Damascus: Writings*, 2.26, trans. Frederic H. Chase, *FC* 37 (Washington: Catholic University of America Press, 1981), 257 [*PTS* 12; 40, 97–98]; On (in)voluntary acts, see Aristotle, *Nicomachean Ethics*, 3.1.1109b 30ff.

32. Diadochos of Photiki, "On Spiritual Knowledge and Discrimination: 100 Texts," 5, in *The Philokalia*, trans. G. Palmer, Philip Sherrard, and Kallistos Ware, vol. 1 (London: Faber & Faber, 1979), 254 [*SC* 5, 5, 86].

33. See Adamantius, *Dialogue on the True Faith in God [de recta in Deum fide]*, 837e/III, 9, trans. Robert A. Pretty, ed. Garry W. Trompf (Leuven: Peeters, 1998), 118–19.

34. Symeon the New Theologian, *Divine Eros: Hymn of St Symeon the New Theologian*, Hymn 53, ll, trans. and ed. Daniel K. Griggs (Crestwood, NY: St. Vladimir's Semi-

nary Press, 2010), 95–144, 375–76; cf. Anestis G. Keselopoulos, *Man and the Environment: A Study of St Symeon the New Theologian*, trans. Elizabeth Theokritoff (Crestwood, NY: St. Vladimir's Seminary Press, 2001).

35. Maximus the Confessor, *Mystagogy*, 7, in *Maximus the Confessor: Selected Writings*, trans. and ed. George C. Berthold (New York: Paulist Press, 1985), 196 (*PG* 91.684D–685A). Here see Lars Thunberg, *Microcosm and Mediator: Theological Anthropology of Maximus the Confessor* (Chicago: Open Court, 1995).

36. Maximus, *On Difficulties in the Church Fathers: The Ambigua* 2:41, ed. and trans. Nicholas Constas (Cambridge, MA: Harvard University Press, 2014), 102–5 (*PG* 91.1304D–1305B).

37. Ibid., 2:41, 105, 109 (*PG* 91.1305C, 1308B).

38. See Irenaeus of Lyons, *AH* Athanasius of Alexandria, *De Incarnatione* in *Contra Gentes and De Incarnatione* 54, II.11–12, ed. and trans. Robert W. Thomson (Oxford: Clarendon, 1971), 268–69; Gregory of Nyssa, *The Great Catechism*, chap. 25 (*PG* 45.65C–68A); Augustine of Hippo, *Sermons (184–229Z) on the Liturgical Seasons*, WSA III/6, trans. Edmund Hil, ed. John E. Rotelle 192.1.1 (New Rochelle, NY: New City Press, 1993), 47; *Expositions of the Psalms, 33–50*, WSA III/16, trans. and ed. Maria Boulding and John E. Rotelle, 49.1.2 (Hyde Park, NY: New City Press, 2000), 381; and Maximus the Confessor, *Ad Thalassium* 22 [*CCSG* 7:137–43], 115–18. For commentary, see Norman Russell, *The Doctrine of Deification in the Greek Patristic Tradition* (Oxford: Oxford University Press, 2004); and David Vincent Meconi, *The One Christ: St. Augustine's Theology of Deification* (Washington, DC: Catholic University of America Press, 2013).

39. See John Zizioulas, *The Eucharistic Communion and the World*, ed. Luke Ben Tallon (London: T&T Clark, 2011), 133–41.

40. See Origen of Alexandria, *On First Principles*, 1.3.6, trans. G. Butterworth (Gloucester: Peter Smith, 1973), 35 [*SC* 252, 154–55, 1.161]; Pseudo-Dionysius the Areopagite, *Divine Names*, in *Pseudo-Dionysius: The Complete Works*, trans. Colm Luibheid, Paul Rorem (New York: Paulist Press, 1987), 5.6 [*PTS* 33; 184, 11.17–21], 99; and Thomas Aquinas, *The Summa Contra Gentiles of St Thomas Aquinas*, 3a.20, trans. English Dominicans (New York: Benziger Brothers, 1924), 38.

41. Maximus the Confessor, *Ambiguum* 7.pref. [*PG* 1068D], 75ff. (exegeting Gregory Nazianzus, *Or.* 14.7 [*PG* 35.865C]).

42. Cyril of Alexandria, *Commentary on John*, I.9, 89c, in Norman Russell, *Cyril of Alexandria* (London: Routledge, 2000), 101.

43. It is not surprising that we see in some of the Christian Fathers the teaching that in time God would have given the human being the Fruit of the Knowledge of Good and Evil. Humankind's sin was then presumption or not waiting on God for His gift of perfection (deification) but seizing it of his own accord before his appointed time (See Ephrem the Syrian, *Hymns on Paradise*, Hymn XII.3, trans. Sebastian Brock (Crestwood, NY: St. Vladimir's Seminary Press, 1990), 161; Section 2, §23, *The Commentary on Genesis* in *Hymns on Paradise*, 214; and Gregory Nazianzus, *Or.* 45.8 (Second Paschal Oration).

44. Irenaeus of Lyons, *Dem.* §22; and see 2 Cor. 4:4.

45. On "priestly garment": "ab Spiritu sanctitatis stolam" (*AH* 3.23.5 and compare 4.20.11).

To Be *Khalīfa*

The Human Vocation in Relation to Nature and Community

MARIA MASSI DAKAKE

IF WE ASK the question, what is humankind's purpose or vocation on earth, the clearest Qur'ānic answer is: to be *khalīfat Allāh fi'l-arḍ*, to be God's representative or vicegerent on earth. Theologically, this is understood to be the ultimate reason for humankind's creation, fall, and exile, and the reason human beings are equipped with intrinsic knowledge as well as guidance from God. It explains why they are entrusted with free will and why other creatures are described as subservient to them. Serving as God's representative to the rest of creation entails a dual responsibility toward both God and creation. But like any viceroy sent to govern territory far from the central authority, humankind is liable to two moral dangers. The first is that they might forget the "delegated" nature of their own authority, abandon the very principles they were charged with establishing and upholding, and create their own arbitrary laws and rules, setting themselves up as petty tyrants whose inflated sense of their own authority is facilitated by forgetting the ultimate source of that authority. The second is that they neglect their duties altogether, becoming enamored of the territory they have been sent to govern. They may grow lazy and complacent, unwilling to undertake the difficulties of maintaining order, and allowing the land to become "overgrown" and chaotic as a result of moral lassitude. The human position as *khalīfa* is certainly understood in Islamic tradition to be a noble one that distinguishes humankind from the rest of creation, but it is, at the same time, one that is beset by a unique set of moral challenges and fraught with moral peril in a way that the Qur'ān rarely lets us forget.

The Qur'ān also makes it clear that the human vocation as *khalīfa*, as God's representative on earth, is a duty that is both individual and collective or universal in nature—a responsibility borne by every human being alone, for which he or she is personally accountable, and by human beings as a whole in relation to the rest of creation. The fact that it is always spoken of as such in the Qur'ān makes it clear that this duty is equally incumbent upon every human being on earth—regardless of gender, race, social status, or any other arbitrary or earthly means of human differentiation, including tribal, ethnic, or even religious communal affiliation. Throughout the Qur'ān, passages dealing with moral responsibility are repeatedly and explicitly discussed in relation to the human being as such (*al-insān*) or to human beings as an undifferentiated species (*al-nās*)—terms that erase all such modes of differentiation and division between them. Since both the origin and the ultimate end of human beings are bound up with this undifferentiated moral vocation, these too are described in the Qur'ān as events that are simultaneously individual and universal in nature. The human species is created metaphorically as a single individual, Adam, whose moral drama, while understood to be that of all human beings, is nonetheless depicted in the Qur'ān as a profoundly personal moral test, shared only by his wife in a parallel and undifferentiated way. In al-A'rāf (7):172, the primordial recognition of God's lordship is voiced simultaneously and *universally* by *all* human souls, but at the same time personally and *individually*, by *each* human soul, thus serving as the metaphysical basis of a very individual conception of human moral responsibility that transcends the narrower religious traditions and affiliations of an individual's family or community in earthly life, as made clear in the very next verse ([7]:173).[1] The Qur'ān also repeatedly informs us that human beings will be resurrected after death just as they were created.[2] That is, they will be resurrected as a collective mass gathered to a universal judgment, on the one hand, but also as individuals profoundly alone as they face their personal reckoning, entirely preoccupied by their own moral fate and necessarily removed and alienated from all of their associates and associations in life, both legitimate and illegitimate.[3]

However, the moral individualism and moral universalism implicit in the Qur'ānic conception of *khalīfa*, or in Qur'ānic descriptions of human origins and otherworldly ends, should not lead us to neglect the very important role that religious community—indeed, the plurality of religious communities—plays in the earthly life of the individual in Qur'ānic discourse. In the Qur'ān, and in the Medinan verses, in particular (for obvious reasons), the establishment of and commitment to a religious community—to the point of building clear boundaries between one's community and those outside of it—is at least an implicit divine mandate, even if the role that such communities play in the moral life of the individual is an ambivalent one. Indeed, the Qur'ān provides us with many examples of prophets and their righteous followers who had to exercise their own moral discernment to challenge or reject the corrupt religious beliefs or practices of the communities into which they were born.[4] Commitment to life in a religious community is thus part of the human vocation according to the Qur'ān, but unlike the vocation to be God's *khalīfa*, it is only a relative and conditional aspect of this vocation, not an absolute one.

In this essay, I begin with a discussion of the well-known Qur'ānic passage in which Adam (and by extension, all humanity) is established as *khalīfat Allāh*

fī'l-arḍ. I focus on the knowledge and status he is given along with this appoint-
ment and what it means that these seemingly great gifts are immediately shown
to be inadequate even to the moral challenges of the paradisal garden, let alone
the challenges of the far more brutal world of earthly exile. From here, I offer a
reading of several Qur'ānic passages that speak to the question of human moral
responsibility and relationship to nonhuman fellow creatures, followed by a discussion of human beings' responsibility to form and maintain moral communities
among themselves.

A Vicegerent on the Earth

> And when thy Lord said to the angels, "I am placing a vicegerent upon
> the earth," they said, "Wilt Thou place therein one who will work
> corruption therein, and shed blood, while we hymn Thy praise and
> call Thee Holy?" He said, "Truly I know what you know not." And He
> taught Adam the names, all of them. Then He laid them before the
> angels and said, "Tell me the names of these, if you are truthful." They
> said, "Glory be to Thee! We have no knowledge save what Thou hast
> taught us. Truly Thou art the Knower, the Wise." He said, "Adam, tell
> them their names." And when he had told them their names, He said,
> "Did I not say to you that I know the unseen of the heavens and the
> earth, and that I know what you disclose and what you once con-
> cealed?" And when We said to the angels, "Prostrate unto Adam,"
> they prostrated, save Iblis. He refused and waxed arrogant, and was
> among the disbelievers. (Baqara [2]:30–34)

This passage is the subject of a good deal of classical and modern commentary,
much of it focusing on the meaning of the "names" taught to Adam by God and
celebrating the hierarchical distinction this knowledge establishes between the
angels and Adam (here representing all humankind). On the basis of this verse,
human beings are considered to be ennobled by this knowledge, making them
superior even to the angels. This widespread interpretation is essential to Islamic
spiritual anthropology and establishes the importance and virtue of knowledge
as intrinsic to human beings' spiritual status and religious lives.[5] The Qur'ānic
account suggests that the knowledge that God teaches to Adam is vast—even
universal—in scope, telling us that God taught Adam "the names, all of them"—a
phrase that has been widely—indeed, almost unanimously—understood to mean
that human beings possess a latent knowledge of *all things*, with the term "names"
understood as a reference to the essences, essential qualities, or realities of all
God's creatures and creations.[6] This knowledge is certainly broad, but does the
Qur'ānic account, in describing this knowledge explicitly as a knowledge of
"names" rather than as the knowledge of "essences" or "realities," suggest that

this knowledge is, as yet, somewhat superficial or that it is not yet very deep or fully understood by its recipient? Adam has indeed learned "the names, all of them," but from another point of view, he has also learned *only* the "names." Having learned the "name" of something, we may have a very sound clue to its essential reality, but often there is still much we have yet to learn about it. Does the account not suggest that Adam may be knowledgeable but not yet wise—that this knowledge implies much potential but one that it is yet unrealized? Adam is a prophet in Islam, and in this capacity, he receives direct knowledge and spiritual status from God. But he is also presented as the first human being, the progenitor of all human beings, and as such serves to encapsulate and represent not only the strengths but also the congenital weaknesses of humanity as whole. To understand the Qur'ānic—and, by extension, Islamic—view of humanity's vocation in the world, therefore, I suggest that we read the story of Adam not only as affirming the nobility of humanity and the human vocation but also as a reminder of humanity's particular flaws and shortcomings, their "clay feet" as it were. In what follows, then, we discuss the Qur'ānic Adam as a representative of humanity as such rather than engaging his status as a prophet.

In the Qur'ānic account, Adam has learned the names of God's creatures and creations well enough to recite them accurately and impressively before the assembled angels. But if we read the story more closely and against the grain of its traditional interpretation, we might be led to wonder what, if anything, Adam has learned about himself in his learning of the names of all things. For example, he knows that he has been "named" *khalīfa*, God's representative on earth, but this title and position is fatefully double-sided. On the one hand, it is a position of honor and nobility, but on the other, it necessarily entails distance and separation from God—for who represents God in His presence? One must wonder whether Adam (and indeed, the human being in general) has comprehended and internalized both aspects of this name and title of *khalīfa*—nobility, but also distance and separation from God? While commentators tend to emphasize the ultimately providential nature of Adam's (humanity's) "fall" and separation from God as a necessary means of fulfilling his spiritual destiny, they overlook the darker and more ominous reality of human exile from God—one that, as the angels seem to know, will indeed entail bloodshed and corruption.[7] The angels may not possess the knowledge God has given specially to Adam, but in this account they do seem to know something about Adam that he has yet to learn about himself.

Moreover, the discourse and behavior of the angels in this account provides a sharp contrast to that of Adam. For while the angels do not possess the expansive knowledge of the "names," which has been given to Adam, they do, in this story, learn something important about themselves, their limits, and their proper place in relation to God and Adam. They acknowledge the limits of their knowledge, their complete dependence on God for whatever knowledge they have, and their status in relation to God's new, favored creature. This self-knowledge on the part of the angels engenders humility, and they bow before Adam as commanded without hesitation. Adam, however, does not seem to have attained a similar degree of self-knowledge in this encounter. On the contrary, we might wonder whether some sense of pride and entitlement has not developed within Adam as a result of his divinely granted honor. Is it not a sense of entitlement that Satan successfully exploits when he encourages Adam to eat from the forbidden tree?

The story of Satan's temptation of Adam is not recounted in the above passage from Sūrat al-Baqara, but in Sūrat al-Aʿrāf (7):19–21 we have an account in which Satan successfully tempts Adam and Eve to eat from the forbidden tree by advising them (disingenuously, of course) that God has forbidden them the tree only to prevent their becoming angels or becoming immortal (7:20). But why are Satan's words so effective in leading Adam and his wife to disobey God? What can Adam stand to gain by becoming an angel—a creature whose knowledge and position has been shown to be inferior to his own? And why should immortality be something to desire when there has been no indication of the possibility of death? Satan's mere suggestion has created in Adam and his wife a sense that there is something they lack and to which they are somehow entitled—beyond the vast gifts of life, knowledge, and sustenance that their Creator has already bestowed upon them. In succumbing to Satan's temptation, Adam and his wife vividly put on display two of the central human flaws for which the Qurʾān repeatedly chastises the human creature: pride and ingratitude. If we read Adam and Eve's disobedience not so much as a sin of desire but one of pride engendered by a sense of entitlement to the angelic status and immortality promised by Satan, then perhaps the story can be read as warning humanity against not only a transgressive material concupiscence but also against a kind of spiritual pride in the status they seem to enjoy—and that the Qurʾān endorses—above all other creatures.

Moreover, Satan's ability to persuade Adam and his wife to eat from the tree by enticing them with benefits they have no reason to believe they do not already enjoy suggests either the inadequacy or incompleteness of the knowledge that they have been given or an inability to use it for their own moral good. In the commentary tradition, one of the reasons that Adam gives for having listened to Satan is that he knew that Satan was one of God's creatures and did not suspect that a creature of God would lie, as when Satan said to Adam: "I am unto thee a sincere adviser" (7:21).[8] Even this excuse, however, indicates an errant reliance upon "names" and suggests that Adam's knowledge thereof is not alone sufficient to meet the challenges he will face as *khalīfa*. Adam also displays his lack of self-knowledge, being unaware of the false sense of entitlement that perhaps makes Satan's particular temptations so effective. Finally, in taking the advice of one of God's creatures over and against God's command, Adam and his wife have already lapsed in their duty as *khalīfa*, for they are meant to serve as the representative of divine command and order, not as seekers of their own desires.

If we read these two Qurʾānic accounts in light of one another, as I have done here, an overly positive interpretation of the passage in which Adam is shown to be superior to the angels in knowledge seems inconsistent with the subsequent events in the garden. The traditional resolution of this apparent conflict in both Judeo-Christian and Islamic contexts is to assert the providential nature of the Fall, which alone permits human beings to realize their full destiny as God's representatives on earth—a resolution that is both theologically sound and morally encouraging and therefore not one to be dismissed. However, I think it is possible to maintain the traditional understanding while also reading against the grain of this traditional interpretation in order to discover a more nuanced conception of Qur'ānic spiritual anthropology, one that, I hope to show, is also borne out by other passages of the Qur'ān that address humanity's moral responsibility and potential.

The Bearer of the "Trust" (Amāna)

Human beings' superiority among God's creatures and their function as *khalīfa* is based upon the notion of their moral responsibility to undertake the burden of obeying God's commands. This moral responsibility logically entails the ability to freely choose moral or immoral actions and to be held accountable accordingly. Here again human beings are distinguished in traditional Islamic cosmology from angels and nonhuman creatures who do not possess free will. It is this human moral accountability (*taklīf*) and a concomitant "free will" that is typically understood to be the meaning of al-Aḥzāb (33):72:[9] "Truly We offered the Trust unto the heavens and the earth and the mountains, but they refused to bear it, and were wary of it—yet man bore it; truly he has proved himself an ignorant wrongdoer."

In this verse, as in the account of Adam just discussed, human superiority is clearly suggested. Human beings have assumed a responsibility that other aspects of God's creation—even those as grand and awe-inspiring as the heavens, the earth, and the mountains—were unwilling to bear. But if this affords human beings any sense of pride at all, the verse's last clause should remind them that this sense of pride is surely misplaced. For all his nobility as God's vicegerent, the human being has proven himself a "wrongdoer" or worse, a "tyrant" (*ẓalūm*); and for all his knowledge of the names of things, he has shown himself to be ignorant (*jahūl*).

While traditional commentators typically understand the first part of al-Aḥzāb (33):72 as an indication of the intelligence and capacity for moral responsibility that human beings alone possess, some interpret this last clause in a more limited fashion as applying only to hypocrites and disbelievers[10]—despite the fact that both parts of the verse concern the same subject: the human being as such. It seems to me that this verse, taken as a whole, embodies the basic human dilemma. Human beings are charged with representing God from a great distance, equipped with a knowledge of themselves and others that is initially superficial and untested.

They are creatures endowed with authority but not wisdom, with knowledge of "the names" but only a partial understanding of their meaning. Human beings have knowledge but must acquire wisdom through testing and experience. Until they acquire it, they cannot exercise authority with justice, nor can their potential to work corruption be held in check. If they succeed in acquiring and applying this wisdom, they will have fulfilled their mission faithfully and perhaps can return from exile; if they fail, the position of *khalīfa* with which they have been entrusted can only condemn them.

Khalīfa in Relation to the Natural World

The idea of humankind as God's *khalīfa fi'l-arḍ* is often understood in a manner very similar to the notion of human beings as the "stewards" of God's earth in the Christian tradition.[11] However, the concept of *khalīfa* differs in two significant respects from the Christian notion of "steward." First, the notion of stewardship in the biblical tradition is derived from a Genesis narrative that also declares the earth to be cursed because of Adam's sin, on account of which it is said that Adam and his descendants will struggle to make the ground yield what they need (Gen. 3:17–19). By contrast, there is no such cursing of the earth or of other creatures on account of Adam's disobedience in the Qur'ānic account. While the Qur'ān indicates that humankind's earthly exile is not the paradisal garden, it nonetheless presents the earth and the rest of creation as full of blessings and designed to serve the myriad needs of God's favored (but imperfect) *khalīfa*. In fact, throughout the Qur'ān the ambivalent moral standing of humankind is explicitly or implicitly juxtaposed and compared to a humble, God-fearing, natural world, which is reliably subservient to both God and humanity.[12] A clear example of this kind of juxtaposition can be found in the opening passage of Sūrat al-Naḥl. In verses 3–7 we read:

> He created the heavens and the earth in truth. Exalted is He above the partners they ascribe. He created man from a drop, and behold, he is a manifest adversary. Cattle has He created for you, in which there is warmth and [other] uses, and whereof you eat. And in them there is beauty for you, when you bring them home, and when you take them out to pasture. And they bear your burdens to a land you would never reach, save with great hardship to yourselves. Truly your Lord is Kind, Merciful.

Here human beings, created from a lowly drop, have dared to set themselves up as a "manifest adversary" to God, and perhaps also to other creatures. And yet in the passage this ominous declaration is immediately followed by a beautiful description of the cattle that God has created, with their many uses for humanity—

from the warmth obtained through their skins and fur, to their nourishing meat, to their service in bearing human beings' (material) burdens. They serve even humanity's aesthetic needs in providing sights of great beauty as they are led out to pasture and brought home again. The passage does not stop there, however; it mentions riding animals, such as horses and mules, that also provide both utilitarian service and a means of "adornment" (al-Naḥl [16]:8); the water from the sky from which vegetation grows ([16]:10–11); the celestial bodies and the earth with its diverse colors ([16]:12–13); the sea that gives food for nourishment, jewels for adornment, and a means of travel ([16]:14); the mountains that provide stability ([16]:15); and finally natural sources of guidance for human beings as they make their way in the world: streams, pathways, stars, and landmarks ([16]:15–16). All this for a "manifest adversary" who struggles to meaningfully reflect on this great bounty.

What can be the meaning or purpose, then, of God's setting up a flawed and prideful human vicegerent over a world of perfect humility and servitude? This brings us the second difference between the Islamic concept of *khalīfa* and Christian concept of stewardship. While the biblical tradition suggests the necessity and importance of human beings tending to God's creation—tilling the paradisal garden, struggling to bring forth the garden from the wilderness in earthly exile, and ultimately delivering the earth from "futility" through their own spiritual redemption (Rom. 8:18–23)[13]—the Qur'ānic text makes it quite clear that the rest of creation, while meant to serve human beings, is spiritual and morally independent of them. It is not ultimately the job of human beings to govern or regulate this natural world, for we are repeatedly reminded that it is God who is in control of its workings and that He has set it perfectly in order. If God's creatures and creations serve human needs, they do so by His command, not ours, according to the Qur'ān. So what is humanity's role in all this, and what does it mean for human beings to be *khalīfa* over a world made continuously blessed and bountiful for them by God's command? For sure, the Qur'ān suggests that human beings are meant to reflect upon all these natural gifts with gratitude and awe and to understand them as signs of God's power and beneficence. But it seems that the human being's duty as *khalīfa* is in large measure a duty to protect this creation from himself and his own potentially destructive and "corrupting" capacities. In al-A'rāf (7):54–56 we read:

> Truly your Lord is God, who created the heavens and the earth in six days, then mounted the Throne. He causes the night to cover the day, which pursues it swiftly; and the sun, the moon, and the stars are made subservient by His Command. Do not creation and command belong to Him? Blessed is God, Lord of the worlds! Call upon your Lord humbly and in secret. Truly He loves not the transgressors. And work not corruption upon the earth after it has been set aright, but

call upon Him in fear and in hope. Surely the Mercy of God is ever nigh unto the virtuous.

Here the human responsibility toward God is to "call upon" Him "humbly and in secret" and not transgress; while humankind's responsibility toward the earth is to avoid corrupting it after it has been set perfectly in order by God. The warning against "working corruption in the earth" is repeated numerous times throughout the Qur'ān, where it is usually understood by traditional commentators to mean that one must avoid the sins of idolatry and disobedience to God's commands, work righteousness, and avoid violence and oppression toward other human beings by establishing and upholding a just and moral social order;[14] the idea that human beings might corrupt the very earth itself or its natural bounties is rarely countenanced by the commentators. However, given that the concept of "working corruption on the earth" is articulated in the cosmological context of the story of the creation of Adam just discussed, and that it is regularly presented as a warning against causing corruption "on earth" rather than more narrowly "in society," "in the community," or "among yourselves," it seems reasonable to suggest that this warning may also pertain to the human potential to corrupt the earth and its natural order—even if commentators living in premodern times could scarcely have imagined the scope of the human potential to destroy the natural world itself that we are all too cognizant of today.[15]

Other Qur'ānic passages allude more directly to the potential for human beings to upset the order and balance of the natural world. This may sometimes result simply from a certain innocent lack of awareness—we might think here of the poor ant in Sūrat al-Naml (27), urging her fellows to get out of the way of Solomon's caravan, lest he crush them in his lack of awareness of their presence ([27]:18–19). Solomon, being a prophet granted the ability to understand the speech of other creatures is of course *not* unaware of the ant, but the story can serve to remind us that ordinary human beings without such extraordinary gifts can hardly know what damage they may do out of lack of awareness. But the human potential for corruption of the natural world may also result from a culpable heedlessness (*ghaflah*, which is contrasted in the Qur'ān to both mindfulness, *taqwā*, and reflection) or from a corruption of their own nature and the betrayal of their duty as *khalīfa*—behaving not as grateful representatives of God but as tyrannical and mutilating overlords toward other creatures. In al-Nisā' (4):118–19, for example, Satan vows to lead human beings toward a much more active manner of corrupting God's creation, saying:

> "Assuredly I will take of Thy servants an appointed share, and surely I will lead them astray, and arouse desires in them. I will command them and they will slit the ears of cattle; I will command them and

they will alter God's creation." Whosoever takes Satan as a protector apart from God has surely suffered a manifest loss.

Here Satan, having already provoked Adam's disobedience and expulsion from the paradisal garden, now takes credit for inspiring human beings to mutilate cattle, the very creatures the Qur'ān has described as a source of natural beauty and myriad benefits for human beings on earth, as we have seen in the passage from Sūrat al-Naḥl, and to "alter God's creation." Such a disfiguration and alteration of God's creatures and creation can be understood only as a satanic inclination and therefore as a "disfiguration" of our own human selves. The premodern commentators do not generally read the passage in this way—the real sin here, they assert, is that these practices are arbitrary rituals devised by human beings as part of pagan religious practices.[16] But to a modern ear, with modern concerns about human manipulations of basic elements of the natural order, a very different reading suggests itself—one that pertains directly to the question of human responsibility to live and behave properly in relation to the natural world—that is, to live within its order and boundaries and not transgress these boundaries by seeking to alter, disfigure, or corrupt its natural beauty.

Human Communities as *khalā'if al-arḍ*

If humanity as a species is God's *khalīfa fi'l-arḍ*, the Qur'ān also identifies human beings as *khalā'if al-arḍ*—vicegerents or successors of one another on the earth. This identification is made in the very last verse of Sūrat al-Anʿām (6), which serves as a kind of prologue to the series of narratives told in the immediately following *sūra* (Sūrat al-Aʿraf) about successive human communities that rejected divine messengers and were consequently collectively destroyed.[17] Taking this as my cue, I argue that part of the human vocation as *khalīfat Allāh fi'l-arḍ* as conceived in the Qur'ān is not only to live righteously and avoid corruption as individuals but also to form human religious communities within which righteous action can be engaged in collectively and hence encouraged, and through the strength of which the forces of human corruption can be kept at bay. Of course, the accounts in Sūrat al-Aʿrāf (7) provide the Qur'ānic reader/listener with spiritually negative examples of "communities"—those that had collectively gone astray—but the fact that the Qur'ān also encourages its audience to construct communities of belief as a shelter from disbelievers and negative spiritual forces suggests that such communities play an important role in the spiritual life of the individual. From one perspective, such communities are merely religious supports for the believers in this world, for the Qur'ān makes it clear that individuals are judged as individuals, independent of their communities, whose collective errors and corruption can serve as no excuse for their individual sins.[18] But from another perspective an individual's salvation is bound up to some extent with the community in which he chooses to be a member, for the Qur'ān also provides us examples of whole communities thrown into hell for their collective moral failings and suggests that individuals are summoned on the Day of Resurrection as members of particular communities ("We shall call every people by their imām"[19]).[20]

Community, from such a perspective, must be understood as a choice rather than as a birthright. Human communities must be found or founded, migrated to, or established so that, ideally, religion can flourish and individuals can be morally sustained, within walls, real or metaphorical, that exclude corrupting influences. The paradigmatic case of the active creation of such a community, of course, is that of the Muslims in Mecca migrating to Medina to build a community where they could practice their religion freely. As difficult as leaving one's home community might be, the Qur'ān presents it as a duty for those living in a place where religion is persecuted:

> When the angels take the souls of those who were wronging themselves, [the angels] say, "In what state were you?" They say, "We were weak and oppressed in the land." [The angels] will say, "Was not God's earth vast enough that you might have migrated therein?" These shall have their refuge in Hell—what an evil journey's end! But not so the [truly] weak and oppressed among the men, women and children, who have neither access to any means nor are guided to any way. As for such, it may be that God will pardon them, for God is Pardoning, Forgiving. Whosoever emigrates in the way of God will find upon the earth many a refuge and abundance, and whosoever forsakes his home, emigrating unto God and His Messenger, and death overtakes him, his reward will fall upon God, and God is Forgiving, Merciful. (al-Nisā' [4]:97–100)

The passage promises both worldly abundance and reward in the Hereafter for those who forsake the comforts of home in order to realize the spiritual possibilities of life in a community grounded in religion, and it threatens otherworldly punishment for those who fail to do so without sufficient excuse. In such ideal communities, as the Qur'ān conceives of them, individual members nourish one another spiritually and aid one another to grow in virtue by commanding right and forbidding wrong to one another through relationships of mutual friendship and protection.[21] The Qur'ān famously suggests in Sūrat al-Mā'ida (5):48 that there may be multiple religious communities who fulfill this function simultaneously and who, though they observe different religious laws and practices, should nonetheless compete with one another in "good deeds." But while virtue and guidance may exist outside a particular religious community or even, perhaps, in multiple communities, this does not negate the religious importance or usefulness of an individual's membership in a clearly defined community. The Qur'ān indicates that there is a special kind of spiritual nurturing that can happen in the context of a religious community with established boundaries and committed membership, even one that excludes others. As we read in Sūrat al-Anfāl (8):72–74

> Truly those who believe, and emigrate, and strive with their wealth and themselves in the way of God, and those who sheltered and helped—they are protectors of one another. As for those who believe and did not emigrate, you owe them no protection until they emigrate. But if they ask your help for the sake of religion, then help is a duty upon you, except against a people with whom you have a covenant. And God sees whatsoever you do. As for those who disbelieve, they are protectors of one another. Unless you do the same, there will be strife (*fitnah*) in the land, and great corruption (*fasād*). As for those who believe, and emigrate, and strive in the way of God, and those who sheltered and helped, it is they who truly are believers. Theirs is forgiveness and a generous provision.

This passage again refers to the situation among the new community in Medina composed of the "emigrants" (*muhājirūn*) and "helpers" (*anṣār*), who are here described as "protecting friends" (*awliyā'*) of one another. The importance of community as a physical entity (at least in this case) is made very stark in this passage, for we see that fellow believers who have not emigrated (to Medina, specifically) do not enjoy a similar relationship of "protecting friendship" with those who have made the effort to form a community there in support of their religion. Although the believers have a duty to help all fellow believers "for the sake of religion," a deeper and more obligating bond is to be established and observed among those who choose to reside in the same community, forsaking their native attachments to do so. To tie one's destiny to fellow believers in a community of faith represents a higher order of religious commitment, and one that comes with additional protections—physical as well as spiritual. The disbelievers, the passage tells us, have established their own communities of mutual protection, and if the believers fail to do the same, it warns, there will be strife (*fitnah*) and great corruption (*fasād kabīr*). Again we have come back to a warning about the potential for human "corruption" on the earth, and the establishment of communities of religious belief is here presented as an important bulwark against our human tendencies in this regard.

Indeed, one might argue that it is not the natural world that needs our vicegerency (*khilāfa*) after all—for the Qur'ān states in Sūrat al-An'ām (6):38 that nonhuman creatures form their own communities (*umam*) and have their own direct relationship with God and forms of worship, and thus seem to be in no need of our governance or mediation with God.[22] First and foremost, our status as *khalīfa* means the responsibility to govern ourselves, to check our own corruptive tendencies, both individually and collectively. This entails, in part, the construction of communities in which our innate goodness can be nurtured and our potential for destruction and corruption held in check. These communal constructs are manmade, however, and as such can be only a relative good—religiously useful and sustaining as long as they are constantly cared for and attended to; but as extensions of our human selves, they are similarly vulnerable to corruption and decay. Moreover, they are temporary, for all such communal barriers are removed on the Last Day when human beings are resurrected all together but at the same time resurrected *as* individuals concerned only with their individual fates. In Sūrat al-Kahf (18), the Qur'ān offers us a dramatic image of the necessity, but temporality, of such human efforts in the account of Dhu'l-Qarnayn:

> Then [Dhu'l-Qarnayn] followed a means, till he reached the place between the two mountain barriers. He found beyond them a people who could scarcely comprehend speech. They said, "O Dhu'l-Qarnayn! Truly Gog and Magog are workers of corruption in the land. Shall we assign thee a tribute, that thou mightest set a barrier between them and us?" He said, "That wherewith my Lord has established me is better; so aid me with strength. I shall set a rampart between you and them. Bring me pieces of iron." Then, when he had leveled the two cliffs, he said, "Blow!" till when he had made it fire, he said, "Bring me molten copper to pour over it." Thus they were not able to surmount it, nor could they pierce it. He said, "This is a mercy from my Lord. And when the Promise of my Lord comes, He will crumble it to dust. And the Promise of my Lord is true." And We shall leave them, on that Day, to surge against one another like waves. And the trumpet shall be blown, and We shall gather them together. (al-Kahf [18]:92–99)

In this Qur'ānic story we are offered the image of the construction of a physical a wall to protect one community against the forces of corruption and destruction embodied in Gog and Magog. The purely human nature of this effort to build a wall is made clear in several ways. First, Dhu'l-Qarnayn is a righteous king in the Qur'ān, and not a prophet, according to most commentators. The decision to build the rampart is presented as a matter undertaken on his own independent initiative rather than one guided by divine instruction. Moreover the graphic, material description of the wall's human construction through the use of iron pieces and molten copper (i.e., materials not naturally found as such in nature but rather materials that can only attained through human industry and processes) reinforces the idea that this is a human effort led by Dhu'l-Qarnayn but requiring the collective efforts of the entire community—note that Dhu'l-Qarnayn asks the community not for payment but for their physical assistance ("aid me with strength"). It is as unclear in the Qur'ān as in the Bible who "Gog" and "Magog" are or what kind of forces they refer to. But the Qur'ānic account in Sūrat al-Kahf

(18) and its classical interpretation in exegetical sources presents them as violent and vicious forces spreading corruption and destruction. One way to read the story symbolically, then, might be to see them as personifications of the violent, corrupting, and destructive tendencies within the human being—individually and collectively—forces that religious communities might (ideally) work together to "wall out" of their societies.

As the righteous human king, Dhu'l-Qarnayn enacts the duty of *khilāfa* with virtuosity and offers us a model of righteous human action in the world—one that is not passive in the face of the presence of evil and corruption—and thus serves as a counterexample to that of those in the earlier passage who tried to excuse their wrongdoing by claiming they were weak and oppressed (*mustaḍʿafūn*) in the land but did not undertake any effort to change their condition. Like the early Muslim emigrants, human beings are called to construct communities of religion and virtue by their own sometimes very physical efforts that can act as a means of restraining their inherently destructive and corruptive tendencies—correctly perceived by the angels, even if this is only half the story. Human beings cannot afford to be either ignorant or passive regarding these inherent tendencies that they bear both individually and collectively; they must strive for greater self-knowledge and understanding and work to actively and continuously protect themselves and the rest of creation from their potential for corruption. But as the Dhu'l-Qarnayn account and other apocalyptic passages in the Qur'ān remind us, all such efforts are but temporary and temporarily useful, for in the end, all humanly constructed barriers and walls—indeed, even the mountains themselves—will be crumbled to dust at the end of time.[23]

Notes

1. The verses read: "And when thy Lord took from the Children of Adam, from their loins, their progeny and made them bear witness concerning themselves, 'Am I not your Lord?' They said, 'Yea, we bear witness'—lest you should say on the Day of Resurrection, 'Truly of this we were heedless,' or lest you should say, '[It is] only that our fathers ascribed partners unto God aforetime, and we were their progeny after them. Wilt Thou destroy us for that which the falsifiers have done?'" (al-Aʿrāf [7]:172–73). This passage is connected with the notion of the human *fiṭra*, the "primordial nature" or "mold" that shapes every human character; see Muḥammad b. Jarīr al-Ṭabarī, *Jāmiʿ al-bayān ʿan taʾwīl āyā al-qurʾān*, vol. 6:9 (Beirut: Dār al-Fikr, 1995), 153–54; Ibn Kathīr, *Tafsīr al-qurʾān al-aʿẓīm*, vol. 2 (Damascus: Dar al-Fīḥāʾ, 1998), 347. *Fiṭra* is the source of the human being's moral responsibility to recognize God's oneness and obey His commands; see al-Qurṭubī, *Tafsīr al-Qurṭubī*, vol. 4 (Cairo: Maktabat al-Īmān, n.d.), 529. Regarding *fiṭra*, see also Sūrat al-Rūm (30):30–31 and al-Qurṭubī's commentary on this verse, al-Qurṭubī, *Tafsīr*, vol. 8, 52–58.

2. See, for example, Sūrat al-Kahf (18):48: "They shall be arrayed before thy Lord in ranks, 'Indeed you have come unto Us as We created you the first time. Nay, but you

claimed that We would never appoint a tryst for you'"; and Sūrat al-An'ām (6):94: "And [God will say,] 'Now you have come unto Us alone, just as We created you the first time, and you have left behind that which We had bestowed upon you. We see not with you your intercessors—those whom you claimed were partners [unto God]. Now the bond between you has been severed, and that which you once claimed has forsaken you.'"

3. See, for example, Sūrat al-Baqara (2):165–66: "Among mankind there are some who take up equals apart from God, loving them as if loving God. But those who believe are more ardent in their love of God. If those who do wrong could but see, when they see the punishment, that power belongs altogether to God and that God is severe in punishment, when those who were followed disavow those who followed, and they see the punishment, while all recourse will be cut off from them"; and Sūrat 'Abasa (80):33–37: "So when the piercing cry does come, that Day when a man will flee from his brother, and his mother and his father, and his spouse and his children. For every man that Day his affair shall suffice him."

4. See Qur'ān 7:59–103, 11:25–99; 26:105–88. The moral heroism involved in challenging and rejecting the practices and traditions of one's native community are, however, most poignantly manifest in the Qur'ānic narratives about Abraham and his people; see 6:74–83; 9:113–14; 19:41–50; 21:51–71.

5. The connection between knowledge and religious nobility is reinforced by the Qur'ān's praise for the "possessors of intellect (*ulu'l-albāb*)" (see Qur'ān 2:269; 3:190–91; and especially 39:9: "Is one who is devoutly obedient during the watches of the night, prostrating and standing [in prayer], wary of the Hereafter and hoping for the Mercy of his Lord. . . . Say, 'Are those who know and those who do not know equal?' Only possessors of intellect reflect."

6. This is the view of most commentators, including very early ones, such as Mujāhid, as recorded by al-Ṭabarī, *Jāmi' al-bayān*, v. 1, pt. 1, 307–15, but also one greatly expanded upon in later philosophical and/or Sufi commentaries, including those of Fakhr al-Dīn al-Rāzī (*al-Tafsīr al-kabīr*, Cairo: n.d., pt. 1, 176–77) and Ibn 'Arabī, *Fuṣūṣ al-ḥikam* (trans. R. W. J. Austin as *The Bezels of Wisdom*, 52–53). The ambivalent referent of the pronoun "*hum*" attached as the direct object of the verb, '*araḍahum* ("He laid *them* before"), which as a masculine plural pronoun, seems to refer to human or at least rational beings, has led to the alternative interpretation that the names that God taught Adam and that he then recited before the angels were the angels' own names, or the names of Adam's progeny—that is, all human beings. al-Ṭabarī favors this interpretation on the basis of the grammatical argument (see al-Ṭabarī, *Jāmi' al-bayān*, v. 1, pt. 1, 310–11). Others, however, suggest that the *hum*, while it does include angels and human beings whose names were taught to Adam, also includes all animate and inanimate, rational and nonrational creations of God, and the masculine plural pronoun is used only because rational creatures like human beings and angels are included among the "things" whose names were taught to Adam. Many early commentators also argue that "the names" taught to Adam refers not only to a knowledge of the names of all things in a superficial sense but also to a knowledge of their essential qualities and attributes, including the benefits that various creatures and creations held for human beings (see al-Ṭabarī, *Jāmi' al-bayān*, v. 1, pt. 1, 309–10). This interpretation is supported by the argument that the Qur'ān's reference to God's "Names" or the "Most Beautiful Names" is understood in Islamic theology to be a reference to God's qualities and attributes (*ṣifāt*).

7. See, for example, Ibn 'Ajībah, *al-Baḥr al-madīd*, on al-A'rāf (7):24–25.

8. See Ibn Kathīr, *al-Tafsīr al-qur'ān al-a'zīm*, v. 2, pp. 275–76; al-Ṭabarī, *Jāmi' al-bayān*, v. 5, 185–86; and al-Zamakhsharī, *al-Kashshāf*, 4 vols. (Beirut: Dār al-Kutub al-'Ilmyyah, 1995), v. 2, 90–92.

9. See al-Qurṭubī, *Tafsīr*, v. 8, 222–26; and Ibn Kathīr, *Tafsīr al-qur'ān al-a'zīm*, v. 3, 689–93. Classical Muslim theologians did not use the phrase "free will" in juxtaposition to predestination. Rather, they discussed it by posing the question of whether moral actions are "created" and, if so, are they not like all things "created by God." They also spoke of "capability" (*istiṭā'ah*) and whether one's capability to perform an act preceded the act itself (thus indicating "free will or free choice") or only existed simultaneously with the performance of the act itself (in which it was divinely predestined). Alternatively, the two positions were sometimes described polemically as a conflict between those who asserted that human beings acted under divine compulsion (*jabr*) and those who held that human beings' ability to engage in morally consequential decision making and action had been given to them as a result of divine delegation (*tafwīḍ*). A compromise position asserted by the majority (Sunnī) Ash'arī school of theology held that, while God determined all things through His decree (*qadar*), human beings do in fact "will" whatever God has already decreed for them and thereby justly incur the moral consequences of their actions through their "acquisition" of responsibility for that action (*iktisāb* or *kasb*).

10. See al-Qurṭubī, *Tafsīr*, v. 8, 222–26.

11. See, e.g., Richard Foltz, "Is There an Islamic Environmentalism?," *Environmental Ethics* 22, (Spring 2000): 64; and Nawwal Ammar, "Islam and Deep Ecology," in *Deep Ecology and World Religions: New Essays on Sacred Grounds*, ed. David Landis Barnhill and Roger S. Gottlieb, 193–212 (Albany: State University of New York Press, 2001), 198.

12. On the ambivalent moral standing of humankind, see, for example, Qur'ān 2:74; 3:83; 5:31; 16:45–50; 19:88–91; 22:18; 24:40–42; 27:82; 41:11–15. On subservience to God and humanity, see, for example, 14:32–33; 22:65; 31:29; 45:12–13.

13. Related to this, see the discussion in E. Calvin Beisner, *Where Garden Meets Wilderness: Evangelical Entry into the Environmental Debate* (Grand Rapids, MI: Eerdmans, 1997), 11–26.

14. See al-Ṭabarī, *Jāmi' al-bayān*, v. 2, 105–6.

15. In this way, we might note with interest a slightly earlier passage in Sūrat al-Baqara ([2]:11), in which the "workers of corruption" on the earth (the *mufsidīn*) reject the charge that they are corrupters, and counter that they are really *muṣliḥūn*, a term generally understood to mean "workers of righteousness," but one that could also mean "improvers" or "reformers"—and, indeed, much of the environmental damage taking place today happens as a result of human attempts to improve or reform the natural world so that it better serves human needs, or at least the needs of a particular set of privileged human beings.

16. al-Zamakhsharī, *al-Kashshāf*, v. 1, p. 526; and al-Ṭabarī, *Jāmi' al-bayān*, v. 4, pt. 6, p. 22.

17. See al-A'rāf (7):59–103.

18. See al-A'rāf (7):173, mentioned above, note 1.

19. Al-Isrā' (17):71. The term "imām" is variously understood to refer to the prophet or scripture one followed in life and thus suggests that people will be resurrected as members of particular religious communities. See al-Qurṭubī, *Tafsīr*, v. 6, p. 251; and al-Ṭabarī, *Jāmi' al-bayān*, v. 9, pt. 15, 157–58.

20. On moral failings, see, for example, al-Aʿrāf (7):38–39.

21. See Sūrat Āl ʿImrān (3):110; and Sūrat al-Tawba (9):71.

22. See al-Isrāʾ (17):44, "The seven heavens, and the earth, and whosoever is in them glorify Him. And there is no thing, save that it hymns His praise, though you do not understand their praise. Truly He is Clement, Forgiving."

23. See, for example, 56:5; 20:105–6.

Scripture Dialogue 2

The Dignity and Task of Humankind within God's Creation

Passages from the Bible

Genesis 1:26–30

[26]Then God said, "Let us make humankind in our image, according to our likeness; and let them have dominion over the fish of the sea, and over the birds of the air, and over the cattle, and over all the wild animals of the earth, and over every creeping thing that creeps upon the earth."

> [27]So God created humankind in his image,
> in the image of God he created them;
> male and female he created them.

[28]God blessed them, and God said to them, "Be fruitful and multiply, and fill the earth and subdue it; and have dominion over the fish of the sea and over the birds of the air and over every living thing that moves upon the earth." [29]God said, "See, I have given you every plant yielding seed that is upon the face of all the earth, and every tree with seed in its fruit; you shall have them for food. [30]And to every beast of the earth, and to every bird of the air, and to everything that creeps on the earth, everything that has the breath of life, I have given every green plant for food." And it was so.

Genesis 2:7–25

[7]then the Lord God formed man from the dust of the ground, and breathed into his nostrils the breath of life; and the man became a living being. [8]And the Lord

God planted a garden in Eden, in the east; and there he put the man whom he had formed. ⁹Out of the ground the Lord God made to grow every tree that is pleasant to the sight and good for food, the tree of life also in the midst of the garden, and the tree of the knowledge of good and evil. ¹⁰A river flows out of Eden to water the garden, and from there it divides and becomes four branches. ¹¹The name of the first is Pishon; it is the one that flows around the whole land of Havilah, where there is gold; ¹²and the gold of that land is good; bdellium and onyx stone are there. ¹³The name of the second river is Gihon; it is the one that flows around the whole land of Cush. ¹⁴The name of the third river is Tigris, which flows east of Assyria. And the fourth river is the Euphrates.

¹⁵The Lord God took the man and put him in the garden of Eden to till it and keep it. ¹⁶And the Lord God commanded the man, "You may freely eat of every tree of the garden; ¹⁷but of the tree of the knowledge of good and evil you shall not eat, for in the day that you eat of it you shall die." ¹⁸Then the Lord God said, "It is not good that the man should be alone; I will make him a helper as his partner." ¹⁹So out of the ground the Lord God formed every animal of the field and every bird of the air, and brought them to the man to see what he would call them; and whatever the man called each living creature, that was its name. ²⁰The man gave names to all cattle, and to the birds of the air, and to every animal of the field; but for the man there was not found a helper as his partner. ²¹So the Lord God caused a deep sleep to fall upon the man, and he slept; then he took one of his ribs and closed up its place with flesh. ²²And the rib that the Lord God had taken from the man he made into a woman and brought her to the man. ²³Then the man said, "This at last is bone of my bones

and flesh of my flesh; this one shall be called Woman,
for out of Man this one was taken." ²⁴Therefore a man leaves his father and his mother and clings to his wife, and they become one flesh. ²⁵And the man and his wife were both naked, and were not ashamed.

Genesis 3:1–13

¹Now the serpent was more crafty than any other wild animal that the Lord God had made. He said to the woman, "Did God say, 'You shall not eat from any tree in the garden'?" ²The woman said to the serpent, "We may eat of the fruit of the trees in the garden; ³but God said, 'You shall not eat of the fruit of the tree that is in the middle of the garden, nor shall you touch it, or you shall die.'"

⁴But the serpent said to the woman, "You will not die; ⁵for God knows that when you eat of it your eyes will be opened, and you will be like God, knowing good and evil." ⁶So when the woman saw that the tree was good for food, and that it was a delight to the eyes, and that the tree was to be desired to make one wise, she took of its fruit and ate; and she also gave some to her husband, who was with

her, and he ate. [7]Then the eyes of both were opened, and they knew that they were naked; and they sewed fig leaves together and made loincloths for themselves. [8]They heard the sound of the Lord God walking in the garden at the time of the evening breeze, and the man and his wife hid themselves from the presence of the Lord God among the trees of the garden. [9]But the Lord God called to the man, and said to him, "Where are you?" [10]He said, "I heard the sound of you in the garden, and I was afraid, because I was naked; and I hid myself." [11]He said, "Who told you that you were naked? Have you eaten from the tree of which I com-manded you not to eat?" [12]The man said, "The woman whom you gave to be with me, she gave me fruit from the tree, and I ate." [13]Then the Lord God said to the woman, "What is this that you have done?" The woman said, "The serpent tricked me, and I ate."

Genesis 9:6–11

> [6]Whoever sheds the blood of a human,
> by a human shall that person's blood be shed;
> for in his own image
> God made humankind.

[7]And you, be fruitful and multiply, abound on the earth and multiply in it.

[8]Then God said to Noah and to his sons with him, [9]"As for me, I am establish-ing my covenant with you and your descendants after you, [10]and with every living creature that is with you, the birds, the domestic animals, and every animal of the earth with you, as many as came out of the ark. [11]I establish my covenant with you, that never again shall all flesh be cut off by the waters of a flood, and never again shall there be a flood to destroy the earth."

Psalm 8

To the leader: according to The Git'tith. A Psalm of David.

[1]O Lord, our Sovereign,

how majestic is your name in all the earth! You have set your glory above the heavens. [2]Out of the mouths of babes and infants you have founded a bulwark because of your foes, to silence the enemy and the avenger. [3]When I look at your heavens, the work of your fingers, the moon and the stars that you have established; [4]what are human beings that you are mindful of them, mortals that you care for them? [5]Yet you have made them a little lower than God, and crowned them with glory and honour. [6]You have given them dominion over

the works of your hands; you have put all things under their feet, ⁷all sheep and oxen,
and also the beasts of the field, ⁸the birds of the air, and the fish of the sea,
whatever passes along the paths of the seas.
⁹O Lord, our Sovereign,
how majestic is your name in all the earth!

Psalm 148

¹Praise the LORD!
Praise the LORD from the heavens;
praise him in the heights
²Praise him, all his angels;
praise him, all his host!
³Praise him, sun and moon;
praise him, all you shining stars!
⁴Praise him, you highest heavens,
and you waters above the heavens!
⁵Let them praise the name of the Lord,
for he commanded and they were created.
⁶He established them for ever and ever;
he fixed their bounds, which cannot be passed.
⁷Praise the Lord from the earth,
you sea monsters and all deeps,
⁸fire and hail, snow and frost,
stormy wind fulfilling his command!
⁹Mountains and all hills,
fruit trees and all cedars!
¹⁰Wild animals and all cattle,
creeping things and flying birds!
¹¹Kings of the earth and all peoples,
princes and all rulers of the earth!
¹²Young men and women alike,
old and young together!
¹³Let them praise the name of the Lord,
for his name alone is exalted;
his glory is above earth and heaven.
¹⁴He has raised up a horn for his people,
praise for all his faithful,
for the people of Israel who are close to him.
Praise the Lord!

Luke 12:22–38

[22]He said to his disciples, "Therefore I tell you, do not worry about your life, what you will eat, or about your body, what you will wear. [23]For life is more than food, and the body more than clothing. [24]Consider the ravens: they neither sow nor reap, they have neither storehouse nor barn, and yet God feeds them. Of how much more value are you than the birds! [25]And can any of you by worrying add a single hour to your span of life? [26]If then you are not able to do so small a thing as that, why do you worry about the rest? [27]Consider the lilies, how they grow: they neither toil nor spin; yet I tell you, even Solomon in all his glory was not clothed like one of these. [28]But if God so clothes the grass of the field, which is alive today and tomorrow is thrown into the oven, how much more will he clothe you—you of little faith! [29]And do not keep striving for what you are to eat and what you are to drink, and do not keep worrying. [30]For it is the nations of the world that strive after all these things, and your Father knows that you need them. [31]Instead, strive for his kingdom, and these things will be given to you as well. [32]Do not be afraid, little flock, for it is your Father's good pleasure to give you the kingdom. [33]Sell your possessions, and give alms. Make purses for yourselves that do not wear out, an unfailing treasure in heaven, where no thief comes near and no moth destroys. [34]For where your treasure is, there your heart will be also.

[35]"Be dressed for action and have your lamps lit; [36]be like those who are waiting for their master to return from the wedding banquet, so that they may open the door for him as soon as he comes and knocks. [37]Blessed are those slaves whom the master finds alert when he comes; truly I tell you, he will fasten his belt and have them sit down to eat, and he will come and serve them. [38]If he comes during the middle of the night, or near dawn, and finds them so, blessed are those slaves."

Romans 1:18–25

[18]For the wrath of God is revealed from heaven against all ungodliness and wickedness of those who by their wickedness suppress the truth.[19]For what can be known about God is plain to them, because God has shown it to them. [20]Ever since the creation of the world his eternal power and divine nature, invisible though they are, have been understood and seen through the things he has made. So they are without excuse; [21]for though they knew God, they did not honor him as God or give thanks to him, but they became futile in their thinking, and their senseless minds were darkened. [22]Claiming to be wise, they became fools; [23]and they exchanged the glory of the immortal God for images resembling a mortal human being or birds or four-footed animals or reptiles. [24]Therefore God gave them up in the lusts of their hearts to impurity, to the degrading of their bodies

among themselves, [25]because they exchanged the truth about God for a lie and worshiped and served the creature rather than the Creator, who is blessed for ever! Amen.

Romans 8:28–30

[28]We know that all things work together for good for those who love God, who are called according to his purpose. [29]For those whom he foreknew he also predestined to be conformed to the image of his Son, in order that he might be the firstborn within a large family. [30]And those whom he predestined he also called; and those whom he called he also justified; and those whom he justified he also glorified.

Romans 12:1–2

[1]I appeal to you therefore, brothers and sisters, by the mercies of God, to present your bodies as a living sacrifice, holy and acceptable to God, which is your spiritual worship. [2]Do not be conformed to this world, but be transformed by the renewing of your minds so that you may discern what is the will of God—what is good and acceptable and perfect.

Ephesians 4:22–24

[22]You were taught to put away your former way of life, your old self, corrupt and deluded by its lusts, [23]and to be renewed in the spirit of your minds, [24]and to clothe yourselves with the new self, created according to the likeness of God in true righteousness and holiness.

Colossians 1:15–20

[15]He is the image of the invisible God, the firstborn of all creation; [16]for in him all things in heaven and on earth were created, things visible and invisible, whether thrones or dominions or rulers or powers—all things have been created through him and for him. [17]He himself is before all things, and in him all things hold together. [18]He is the head of the body, the church; he is the beginning, the firstborn from the dead, so that he might come to have first place in everything. [19]For in him all the fullness of God was pleased to dwell, [20]and through him God was pleased to reconcile to himself all things, whether on earth or in heaven, by making peace through the blood of his cross.

1 John 3:1–3

¹See what love the Father has given us, that we should be called children of God; and that is what we are. The reason the world does not know us is that it did not know him. ²Beloved, we are God's children now; what we will be has not yet been revealed. What we do know is this: when he is revealed, we will be like him, for we will see him as he is.³And all who have this hope in him purify themselves, just as he is pure.

Passages from the Qurʾān[1]

Al-Baqara (2):30–34

³⁰And when thy Lord said to the angels, "I am placing a vicegerent upon the earth," they said, "Wilt Thou place therein one who will work corruption therein, and shed blood, while we hymn Thy praise and call Thee Holy?" He said, "Truly I know what you know not." ³¹And He taught Adam the names, all of them. Then He laid them before the angels and said, "Tell me the names of these, if you are truthful."

³²They said, "Glory be to Thee! We have no knowledge save what Thou hast taught us. Truly Thou art the Knower, the Wise." ³³He said, "Adam, tell them their names." And when he had told them their names He said, "Did I not say to you that I know the unseen of the heavens and the earth, and that I know what you disclose and what you used to conceal?"

³⁴And when We said to the angels, "Prostrate unto Adam," they prostrated, save Iblis. He refused and waxed arrogant, and was among the disbelievers.

Al-Naḥl (16):3–17

³He created the heavens and the earth in truth. Exalted is He above the partners they ascribe. ⁴He created man from a drop, and behold, he is a manifest adversary. ⁵And cattle has He created for you, in which there is warmth and [other] uses, and whereof you eat. ⁶And in them there is beauty for you, when you bring them home, and when you take them out to pasture. ⁷And they bear your burdens to a land you would never reach, save with great hardship to yourselves. Truly your Lord is Kind, Merciful. ⁸And [He has created] horses, mules, and asses, that you may ride them, and as adornment, and He creates that which you know not. ⁹And it is for God to show the way, for some of them lead astray. Had He willed, He would have guided you all together. ¹⁰He it is Who sends down water from the sky, from which you have drink, and from which comes vegetation wherewith you pasture your cattle. ¹¹Therewith He causes the crops

to grow for you, and olives, and date palms, and grapevines, and every kind of fruit. Truly in that is a sign for a people who reflect. ¹²He has made the night and the day subservient unto you, and the sun, and the moon, and the stars are subservient by His Command. Truly in that are signs for a people who understand. ¹³And whatsoever He created for you on the earth of diverse colors—truly in this is a sign for a people who reflect. ¹⁴He it is Who made the sea subservient, that you may eat fresh meat therefrom, and extract from it ornaments that you wear. You see the ships plowing through it, and [this is so] that you may seek His Bounty, and that haply you may give thanks. ¹⁵And He cast firm mountains into the earth, lest it shake beneath you, and streams, and ways, that haply you may be guided, ¹⁶and landmarks, and by the stars they are guided. ¹⁷Is He Who creates like one who creates not? Will you not, then, reflect?

Al-Nisāʾ (4):132–35

¹³²Unto God belongs whatsoever is in the heavens and whatsoever is on the earth, and God suffices as a Guardian. ¹³³If He so wills, He can remove you, O mankind, and bring others [in your stead], and God has full power to do so. ¹³⁴Whosoever desires the reward of this world, with God is the reward of this world and the Hereafter. God is Hearing, Seeing. ¹³⁵O you who believe! Be steadfast maintainers of justice, witnesses for God, though it be against yourselves, or your parents and kinsfolk, and whether it be someone rich or poor, for God is nearer unto both. So follow not your caprice, that you may act justly. If you distort or turn away, truly God is Aware of whatsoever you do.

Al-Aḥzāb (33):70–72

⁷⁰O you who believe! Reverence God and speak justly, ⁷¹that He may set your deeds to aright for you, and forgive you your sins. And whosoever obeys God and His Messenger has achieved a great triumph. ⁷²Truly We offered the Trust unto the heavens and the earth and the mountains, but they refused to bear it, and were wary of it—yet man bore it; truly he has proved himself an ignorant wrongdoer.

Al-Aʿrāf (7):54–58

⁵⁴Truly your Lord is God, Who created the heavens and the earth in six days, then mounted the Throne. He causes the night to cover the day, which pursues it swiftly; and the sun, the moon, and the stars are made subservient by His Com-

mand. Do not creation and command belong to Him? Blessed is God, Lord of the worlds! ⁵⁵Call upon your Lord humbly and in secret. Truly He loves not the transgressors. ⁵⁶And work not corruption upon the earth after it has been set aright, but call upon Him in fear and in hope. Surely the Mercy of God is ever nigh unto the virtuous. ⁵⁷He it is Who sends forth the winds as glad tidings ahead of His Mercy, so that when they bear heavy-laden clouds, We may drive them toward a land that is dead, and send down water upon it, and thereby bring forth every kind of fruit. Thus shall We bring forth the dead, that haply you may remember. ⁵⁸As for the good land, its vegetation comes forth by the leave of its Lord. And as for the bad, it comes forth but sparsely. Thus do We vary the signs for a people who give thanks.

Al-Nisāʾ (4):97–100

⁹⁷When the angels take the souls of those who were wronging themselves, [the angels] say, "In what state were you?" They say, "We were weak and oppressed in the land." [The angels] will say, "Was not God's earth vast enough that you might have migrated therein?" These shall have their refuge in Hell—what an evil journey's end! ⁹⁸But not so the [truly] weak and oppressed among the men, women, and children, who have neither access to any means nor are guided to any way. ⁹⁹As for such, it may be that God will pardon them, for God is Pardoning, Forgiving. ¹⁰⁰Whosoever migrates in the way of God will find upon the earth many a refuge and abundance, and whosoever forsakes his home, emigrating unto God and His Messenger, and death overtakes him, his reward will fall upon God, and God is Forgiving, Merciful.

Al-Anfāl (8):72–75

⁷²Truly those who believe, and migrate, and strive with their wealth and themselves in the way of God, and those who sheltered and helped—they are protectors of one another. As for those who believe and did not migrate, you owe them no protection until they migrate. But if they ask your help for the sake of religion, then help is a duty upon you, except against a people with whom you have a covenant. And God sees whatsoever you do. ⁷³As for those who disbelieve, they are protectors of one another. Unless you do the same, there will be a strife in the land, and a great corruption. ⁷⁴As for those who believe, and migrate, and strive in the way of God, and those who sheltered and helped, it is they who truly are believers. Theirs is forgiveness and a generous provision. ⁷⁵As for those who believe after you and migrate and strive with you, they are [to be counted] among you. But family relations have the strongest claim on one another in the Book of God. Truly God is Knower of all things.

Al-Kahf (18):92–99

[92]Then [Dhu'l-Qarnayn] followed a means, [93]till he reached the place between the two mountain barriers. He found beyond them a people who could scarcely comprehend speech. [94]They said, "O Dhu'l-Qarnayn! Truly Gog and Magog are workers of corruption in the land. Shall we assign thee a tribute, that thou mightest set a barrier between them and us?" [95]He said, "That wherewith my Lord has established me is better; so aid me with strength. I shall set a rampart between you and them. [96]Bring me pieces of iron." Then, when he had leveled the two cliffs, he said, "Blow!" till when he had made it fire, he said, "Bring me molten copper to pour over it." [97]Thus they were not able to surmount it, nor could they pierce it. [98]He said, "This is a mercy from my Lord. And when the Promise of my Lord comes, He will crumble it to dust. And the Promise of my Lord is true." [99]And We shall leave them, on that Day, to surge against one another like waves. And the trumpet shall be blown, and We shall gather them together.

Note

1. Seyyed Hossein Nasr et al., eds., *The Study Quran: A New Translation and Commentary* (New York: HarperOne, 2015).

PART IV

Human Action within the Sovereignty of God

Human Freedom and Divine Sovereignty

Muslim Perspectives

FERAS Q. HAMZA

IN MUSLIM THEOLOGICAL discourse, the terms used to discuss the question of free will versus divine predetermination did not directly emerge from the Qur'ānic lexicon, though concepts such as God's decree and preordainment (*al-qaḍā' wa'l-qadar*), specifically in conjugated expressions such as *qaddara Allāh* or *qaḍa Allāh*, are well-known Qur'ānic refrains. To a large extent, from as early as the mid-second/eighth century, the theological discourse coalesced around a number of technical terms that were simply the obvious Arabic vernacular for the concepts and questions implied by the main topic: terms such as *jabr* (compulsion), *tafwīḍ* (delegation), *iktisāb* (acquisition), *ikhtiyār* (choice), or *istiṭā'a* (capacity) do not appear in the Qur'ān, either in substantive or verbal form, in any obviously related way to the theme of free will and predestination.[1] Indeed, the term that would come to denote the adherents of "free will," *ahl al-qadar*, is a term that in the Qur'ān (and, indeed, in the Arabic language generally) implies quite the opposite—namely "fate" or "destiny"—hence, more on the side of pre-determination. Of course, the point here is not that one would expect to find a theology of free will or predetermination in the Qur'ān but then does not. All that one could find in the Qur'ān was support for both positions. It is that, from very early on, the scriptural narrative itself, taken in its entirety, must have stimulated and fed the devotional imagination of the pious to ponder this question using everyday language. But before elaborating on this important link between scripture, theology, and devotion, a brief historical prelude is needed.

It is important to note that the theological debate over free will and predetermination in the early period was firmly anchored in, and in large measure precipitated by, intra-Muslim religious polemics over urgent political questions. Indeed, political context of, or the political background against which, theological questions were raised is usually taken by granted for Islamicists, given the religiopolitical symbiosis that characterized the birth of the Prophet's community, which in turn became the early Muslim polity of seventh-century Arabia. Be that as it may, the tendency to explain away early theological concerns as merely political statements tends to overlook the fact that theology was also very personalist and devotional. From the time of nineteenth-century scholars such as Ignaz Goldziher right up to the time of later ones such as Montgomery Watt, Josef van Ess, and Michael Cook, most Islamicists have emphasized the political nature of these theological debates, pointing out that the Umayyads were determinists, or predestinarians, while their opponents were *qadarīs*, or advocates of free will, or that the theological debate mostly provided the terms of reference for political struggle. But in fact, there never seems to have been a neat divide with those in political office favoring a predestinarian outlook while their opponents were all supporters of free will (for God could clearly have predestined that rebels overturn those in office and so on, ad infinitum). Indeed, the political opponents of the Umayyads were themselves mostly on the "fatalistic" side: Kharijites, Murji'ites, and Shi'ites were all in the early period determinists.[2]

The notion that a particular theological position was mostly a foil for political aspirations arises from a not altogether unjustified distrust of the historicity of what were considered "deviant" or heterodox theologies as portrayed by the Muslim heresiographical (*firaq*) literature: Islamicists were naturally skeptical about the historicity of various entries in these heresiographical traditions because the heresiographers themselves so schematically made use of what was emerging as their own orthodox theology to anathematize, so to speak, nonaffiliates or members of other Muslim communities. A typical heresiographical work was structured around a series of theological topics (*qaḍā wa'l-qadar, imāma, ru'yat Allāh, al-ṣifāt, al-khurūj min al-nār*), and individuals or sectaries were named (and shamed) according to the position that they were said to have held on each of these topics. So we find that the origin of the idea of *qadar* (free will) is associated with Ma'bad al-Juhanī (d. 80/699), who was executed by the Umayyad governor al-Ḥajjāj (d. 95/714) for his part in the anti-Umayyad revolt of Ibn al-Ash'ath in the year 82/701. In two separate studies, Suleyman Murad (1991) and Michael Cook (1981) explain that it was because of his role in the revolt and not because of his Qadarism that Ma'bad was eventually executed. Likewise, Ghaylan al-Dimashqi (d. *post* 105/723), whom the Muslim heresiographical tradition associates with the Qadariyya (the proponents of "free will"), was also executed by the Umayyads, and again we are told by Islamicists, not on account of his Qadarism but for clashing with the Umayyad authorities during the reign of Hishām b. 'Abd al-Malik.

Clearly, by the time the Muslim heresiographical tradition (850–1000) was coming together (as a literary genre if nothing else), many questions had been settled, or at least Muslim heresiographers had settled on theological positions that reflected their worldviews and what was considered "best" for their respective communities—in other words, what would in effect constitute orthodoxy. I think that it is worth emphasizing this social context: the concern for public morality in many ways stunted the potential for further theological development; or, one might say, the concern for public order, the rule of law, the legitimacy of the caliphal institution, and the psychospiritual health of the community, certainly for the majoritarian ulama, who were the mostly Sunnī traditionalists, all necessitated a theology that kept individuals clear of the moral anxiety of particular theological questions and clear of any scandalous reaction. Because it seemed that armed with the "right" theology, you could mount a rebellion, become schismatic (Kharijites), or even suspend the Law (Ismāʿilī Qarmatis) as several strains of *ghulāt* proto-Shiʿism or pre-Imamism in the formal sense as well as pre-Fatimid Ismāʿilīsm did.[3] This is not to suggest, of course, that theology ends with the emergence of the main orthodoxies, whether Sunnī or Shiʿī.[4]

In fact, my argument is that productive theology from the outset was a devotional impulse: what the earliest theological treatises show us is that the first real theologians were themselves paragons of piety. Al-Ḥasan al-Baṣrī (d. 110/728), as a key early ascetic figure, and Muḥammad b. al-Ḥasan b. al-Ḥanafiyya (d. 81/700) are but two examples. Even someone like Aḥmad Ibn Ḥanbal (d. 241/855), who had as many admirers as his school of thought has since had detractors, is said to have authored a *Kitab al-zuhd* (Asceticism).[5]

Support for both sides of the argument surrounding God's predetermination of events and man's free will—notwithstanding the qualification made at the beginning of this essay that most of the technical lexicon of the free will debate issued from extra-Qurʾānic discussions—were naturally sought within the revelation. And it is fair to say that both the advocates of predestination (*jabr*) and the proponents of free will (*qadar*) could find scriptural basis for their respective views. This seeming dichotomy to some extent reflects the Qurʾān's reiteration of God's absolute sovereignty and, at the same time, its insistence on man's God-given power to choose his path in life and to reap the reward thereof accordingly: in fact, the whole system of reward and punishment could only be premised on God's essential attribute of justice. And so, as al-Kahf (18):29 tells us, "Let he who wishes [to do so] believe, and let he who wishes [to do so] disbelieve" (*fa-man shāʾa faʾl-yuʾmin wa-man shāʾa faʾl-yakfur*).[6] Such a statement conformed, in general, with the spirit of God's admonitions to mankind in the Qurʾān—that is to say, with the idea that man would be requited only according to his deeds and that God does not charge any soul except with what it can bear (al-Baqara [2]:286). Indeed, in numerous instances God assures people that He would never do injustice (*ẓulm*) to them, not even so much as "a single date-thread" (al-Nisāʾ [4]:49, *wa-lā yuẓlamūna fatīlan*), or in another expression, not so much as "the speck on a date-stone" (al-Nisāʾ [4]:124, *wa-lā yuẓlamūna naqīran*). The reason God created the heavens and the earth, says al-Jāthiyah (45):22, was so that every person would be recompensed according to their deeds. The logical implication from all of this—namely, that God was not unjust and that man would be requited only according to his deeds—was that man was essentially free to choose his actions. That was the famous position adopted by the earliest advocates of rationalist reasoning (*ahl al-ra'y*) in Islam, the Mu'tazila. Indeed, one of the main arguments used by the Mu'tazila to support their view and to refute the view of their mainly Sunnī traditionalist (*ahl al-ḥadīth*) opponents— who insisted on Divine predestination—was precisely that it was absurd and unjust that God should make promises of reward and threats of punishment to mankind, then charge them with religious obligations (*taklīf*) if their individual destinies had already been decreed before they were even born. It was for this reason that the Mu'tazila labeled such traditionalists *mujbira* or *jabriyya*, literally "those in favor of coercion." The Mu'tazila and other proponents of human "free will" came to be known, somewhat illogically, as *qadariyya* or *ahl al-qadar*. Returning to the Qur'ān, however, it should also be noted that those who were opposed to human free will and insisted on God's absolute determination of all events could also find support for this view in both the scripture and, far more significantly, the body of ḥadīth material (the Prophetic traditions). Perhaps somewhat mistakenly, many verses describing God's all-encompassing knowledge and God's "leading men astray" (*aḍalla, yuḍillu*) were taken by traditionalist scholars to be proof that God predetermines all things. In fact, later more sophisticated arguments in both 'ilm al-kalām and *falsafa* would reiterate arguments that God's foreknowledge of events did not necessarily determine them. Moreover, on the subject of *iḍlāl*, where the Qur'ān makes statements such as "Do you wish to guide those whom God has led astray?" (al-Nisā'[4]:88; see also Ibrāhīm [14]:4; and al-Rūm [30]:29), one might argue that the meaning of the Arabic *aḍalla* is not "He leads them astray" but "He leaves them to go astray." In other words, God does not intervene to guide them to the right path once they have chosen the path of error or misguidance. This notion is suggested by the very fact that those whom God wishes that they be saved enjoy His grace (*luṭf*) and then providence (*'ināya*). The opposite of Divine providence would be banishment or abandonment, which is tantamount to perdition, since that person can no longer hope for God's guidance. Despite all of this, there were many ḥadīths that suggested that certain key features of an individual's earthly sojourn were preordained, precisely his moment of birth, a source of sustenance or provision (*rizq*), his term of life and his moment (and place of death). But also, somewhat problematically, we find, as in the well-known ḥadīth of the "womb" (Bukhārī, Ṣaḥīḥ, bāb al-qadar, 82) that every child, while still in its mother's womb, has its fate recorded by an angel either as fortunate (*sa'īd*) or damned (*shaqī*). To be clear, this is just one among many traditions that were already circulating in the second/eighth century and that suggested a strong tendency toward or preference for a predestinarian theology in early Islam.[7]

The importance of the *qadarī* movement, however, lies not in its early political associations but in its contribution to the formation of the theological school of the Mu'tazila in Basra. The exponents of *qadar* can, to a certain extent, be identified as the proto-Mu'tazila of the early second century, a movement whose beginnings could be traced to the circle of students around the famous early ascetic al-Ḥasan al-Baṣrī. In fact, the earliest extant document for the contro-versy over the question of *qadar* as "free will" comes from an epistle written by al-Ḥasan al-Baṣrī to the Umayyad caliph ʿAbd al-Malik b. Marwān (d. 86/705). The views expounded by al-Ḥasan here represent a transition from the tradition-alist stance of *jabr* to what would later become the Muʿtazilī position on human free will: al-Ḥasan was essentially arguing that the bad deeds of human beings were from themselves while the good deeds were from God.[8] Gradually the shift toward humanity's freedom to do both good and evil and thus be morally respon-sible for his behavior would become complete, primarily as a result of the ideas of scholars such as ʿAmr b. ʿUbayd (d. 144/761), a student of al-Ḥasan, and Wāṣil b. ʿAṭāʾ (d. 131/748), both of whom would later be adopted by Muʿtazilīs as the founders of the Muʿtazilī movement in Basra. For the Muʿtazila school, the con-cept of human free will, or *qadar*, would come to constitute the foundation of one of their five principal tenets (*al-uṣūl al-khamsa*): God's justice (ʿ*adl*). Because God is just, He would only punish humans for evil actions, which they have performed of their own free choice.

The other principal development in the history of *jabr* and *qadar* is associ-ated with the famous scholar, and eponym of the later theological school, Abūʾl-Ḥasan al-Ashʿarī (d. 324/935). He was originally a Muʿtazilī—his teacher was Abū ʿAlī al-Jubbāʾī (d. 303/915), the head of the Basran school of the Muʿtazila—but came to reject this school of thought and devoted major works to refuting their tenets. Now, however, he would polemicize against them by adopting their own rationalist dialectical techniques. In his famous work *al-Ibāna ʿan uṣūl al-diyāna* he makes a crucial distinction regarding the question of *jabr* and *qadar*—namely, that all acts are created (*khalq*) by God while it is man who acquires (*kasb, iktisāb*) them by his own free will; God has empowered (*tafwīḍ*) mankind with the capacity (*istiṭāʿa*) to make that free choice (*ikhtiyār*). In fact, the origins of this concept of acquisition (*kasb*) can be traced back earlier to the Baṣran Muʿtazilī Ḍirār b. ʿAmr (d. ca. 200/815) and even, arguably, to the famous Imāmī *mutakallim* Hishām b. al-Ḥakam (d. 179/795). Simply put, Ḍirār stated that God creates the act while man acquires it.[9] Hishām, on the other hand, sought to bring out the distinction between *compulsion* and *choice* by stating, in addition to all acts being the creation of God, that one's acts constitute a "choice" (*ikhtiyār*) for oneself, in one sense, and "compulsion" (*iḍṭirār*), in another—"choice" in that one wills and acquires them; "compulsion" in that they issue from a person only when the necessitating cause (*sabab*) comes into being.[10] Hence-forth, the term *ikhtiyār* appears more frequently, though not consistently, in sophisticated theological and philosophical discussions about the nature of human agency.[11]

What has defined this question ever since, including in this modern age, has been the effort to reconcile God's omnipotence with man's perceived freedom of action (now more often referred to as *ḥurriyya*). Thus, the late Lebanese *marjaʿ* Sayyid Muḥammad Ḥusayn Faḍl Allāh (d. 2010) offered the following summary of the question in his commentary on al-Qamar (54):49 *innā kulla shay'in khalaqnāhu bi-qadar* ("Every thing We have created according to a measure"):

> *Qadar* is not limited to cosmic phenomena, but extends also to the movement of human existence in its entirety. There are [established] divine laws that govern the movement of (both) the individual human and societies, from their inception to their demise. Choice (*ikhtiyār*) is one of the elements contained in these established ways. Belief in (God's omnipotent) power (*qudra*) does not preclude human will, since the meaning of (God's omnipotent) power is [that He] defines the movement of existence and designs its conditions (*shurūṭ*), so that choice is part of this measure (*qadar*), given that it is included in the divine way (ordained) for the movement of existence.[12]

The question of free will and divine determinism, as has been noted in much contemporary theological discussion, transcends "reason" as the process of ratiocination. In other words, such a question is not one amenable to resolution, let alone by any Aristotelian logic of noncontradiction. For the question itself— better, the mystery—is really no more than an extension of the larger mystifying but dynamic relationship between the divine and the human, reason and revelation, prophetic and rational discourse, transcendence and immanence, the infinite and the finite, the temporal and the atemporal, and so on, in an endless list of widely acknowledged binaries. But this mysterious relationship is precisely what animates religious devotions. The Prophet is said to have referred his companions Abu Bakr and Umar, who were hotly discussing the issue of free will and divine predestination, to the symbolic figure of a mighty angel. He explained that this angel is of a highly paradoxical constitution, being half fire and half ice, so that the fire neither melts the ice nor the ice extinguishes the fire; yet this angel praises its Maker for maintaining it in existence. Hence, from our vantage point, events are ever unfolding even as they are surely accomplished from God's vantage point, if one can use that term. In fact, in another version, Umar asks the Prophet if the matter is already accomplished, what is the meaning of action. To that, the Prophet replies, "Act, O Umar! For, every creature is eased towards that for which it has been created."[13] Clearly, seventh-century sensibilities could be theologically engaged and theologically satisfied by such a paradoxical response. One must then contend with the very nature of paradox.[14] After all, human beings are a truth and so, for the faithful, is God. The human condition is a truth, but so also the possibility of apo*theosis*. Held together, these two truths are dynamic: they can be understood as complementarities if not thought of as productive contrarieties. Systematic theology cannot satisfy, which is why a theology unanchored in devotional practice is at best dry, at worst frustrating. Devotions should underpin any theological question. For what cannot be resolved by the mind is surely better laid to rest by the heart: "Nothing but supplication can ward off preordained [God's] judgement" (*lā yaruddu al-qaḍāʾ illā al-duʿāʾ*).[15]

What can one take from this debate over free will and predestination? Faced with this theological conundrum, could a believer truthfully favor one over the other? The choice seems impossible, for neither option is bearable ontologically. Or should the question be thought of differently? It would seem closer to the empirical reality of the believer's journey through life to see human agency and divine sovereignty in terms of the following exchange between Moses and Pharaoh in the Qurʾān:

> Pharaoh asked, "Who then is this Lord of yours, O Moses?" Said he [Moses]: "Our Lord is the One who gave every living thing its particular form then proceeded to guide [it]." (Ṭā-Hā [20]:49–50)

The believer is enjoined to consecrate this journey through life by bringing the divine presence into all moments, inviting this presence by active devotion so that agency and divine sovereignty come together as one harmony.

> And when My servants question you concerning Me, I am near: I answer the call of the caller when he calls to Me; so let them respond to Me, and let them believe in Me that they might go aright. (al-Baqara [2]:186)

Notes

1. Regarding *iktisāb*, of course, the root itself, *k-s-b*, makes frequent enough appearance in the Qurʾān to denote an individual's agency and to imply responsibility at the time of the Final Judgement. However, the technical Ashʿarite term does not appear until two centuries later (Ashʿarī d. 324/923). The same is true of the verbal noun *istiṭāʿa*.

2. Twelver Imamī Shiʿism would later flourish under heavy Muʿtazilī (free will) influence, but for that one has to wait at least two centuries. On the Shīʿa, see Asaf A. A. Fyzee, *A Shīʿite Creed* (Oxford: Oxford University Press, 1942) for an early creed; and see M. J. McDermott, *The Theology of Shaikh al-Mufīd (d. 413/1022)* (Beirut: Dar el-Machreq, 1978) for the mature classical position.

3. Perhaps this early conservatism stunted the potential for elaborate discussions of morality and prevented the flowering of a field of Muslim ethics (a mostly contemporary phenomenon).

4. See, for example, Josef van Ess, "The *kalam* phenomenon reached its zenith very early; its most creative period did not occur after it had come of age, but well before, at a time when signs of tedium and paralysis had not yet appeared." Josef van Ess, *The Flowering of Muslim Theology* (Cambridge, MA: Harvard University Press, 2006), 4.

5. Contemporary Salafism and Wahhabī theologians both draw inspiration from the teachings of the medieval Ibn Taymiyya (d. 1328), who was a sophisticated Ḥanbalī juris-

prudent (on whom, for this question, see J. Hoover, *Ibn Taymiyya's Theodicy of Perpetual Optimism* [Leiden: Brill, 2007]).

6. Regarding Qur'ān translations, I have principally drawn on the as yet unsurpassed translation of Ali Quli Qara'i, *The Qur'an: With a Phrase-by-Phrase English Translation* (London: ICAS Press, 2004); but ultimately, all translations are my own.

7. See, for instance, W. Montgomery Watt, *Free Will and Predestination in Early Islam* (London: Luzak, 1948).

8. On all of this, see Michael Cook, *Early Muslim Dogma: A Source-Critical Study* (Cambridge: Cambridge University Press, 1981).

9. Ash'arī, *Maqālāt*, 281.

10. Ash'arī, *Maqālāt*, 40ff.; see, for example, W. Montgomery Watt, *The Formative Period of Islamic Thought* (Edinburgh: Edinburgh University Press, 1973).

11. For example, Ibn Sīnā (d. 429/1037), in his *al-Shifā'* (*al-Ilāhiyyāt*; see also *al-Najāt*); and al-Ghazālī (d. 505/1111), in his *Iḥyā' 'ulūm al-dīn* (*Kitāb qawā'id al-'aqā'id: al-rukn al-thalith*).

12. *Min waḥy al-Qur'ān*, vol. 21, 295.

13. For an important discussion of this report, see T. Mayer, *Keys to the Arcana: Shahrastānī's Esoteric Commentary on the Qur'an* (Oxford: Oxford University Press, 2009), 113–18.

14. See, for example, D. R. Stiver, *Ricoeur and Theology* (London: Bloomsbury, 2012); and Paul Ricoeur, *Freedom and Nature: The Voluntary and the Involuntary*, trans. E. V. Kohak (Chicago: Northwestern University Press, 1966).

15. A well-known Prophetic admonition often repeated by imāms just before the Friday congregational prayer as part of the concluding supplications that come between the end of the sermon and immediately before prayer commences. For numerous examples of this Muslim attitude in devotions, see Constance E. Padwick, *Muslim Devotions: A Study of Prayer-Manuals in Common Use* (London: SPCK, 1961).

Human Action within the Sovereignty of God

Christian Perspectives

VELI-MATTI KÄRKKÄINEN

TO MAKE MY discussion of human action within the sovereignty of God manageable and useful for this particular occasion, I limit its scope in significant ways. I do not seek to respond to the denial of human freedom by those natural scientists to whom world processes are deterministic to the point of eliminating any true notion of freedom. Nor do I take up the equally strong rejection of human freedom by neuroscientists and philosophers of mind who argue that everything humans do is caused by our "neurons"—that is, neuroscientific determinism. I have discussed and defeated these forms of determinism elsewhere and simply assume here the commonsense notion of human freedom.[1] As limited as it may be (because there are so many givens in human life beginning from gender, birthplace, and ethnicity), it is also so obvious and intuitive that even freedom's deniers, luckily, do not live according to their belief; even the most hard-core neuroscientist determinists hardly oppose sentencing a serial killer or a child molester.[2] Similarly—and curiously—even the most deterministic scientific accounts are often prefaced by passing remarks on the necessity of free will for a meaningful personal or social life.[3] Finally, I exclude from my considerations the matrix of complicated philosophical and theological issues concerning the meaning and conditions of free will, networked with a number of problems from moral agency and responsibility to compulsion, addiction, and weakness of will, to criminal punishment, all the way to a number of metaphysical issues.[4] Let it suffice to clarify the meaning of the term "freedom" by merely raising the most basic question of whether a person is able to act as one chooses without compulsion or whether one is able to choose freely. My shorthand response is this: I speak of freedom in terms of both freedom *from* compulsion (of any sort) and freedom *for* making meaningful choices.[5]

My aim is theological. In keeping with the suggestive thematic questions given here, I seek to clarify from the perspective of Christian tradition the following interrelated themes: What are the implications of the common Christian and Islamic conviction that humans act within a Creation that is to a large extent given and that we also act in relationship to the sovereign Creator who is even now at work? Or to put it a little bit differently: Human freedom—real or illusory? Illusory because we are determined by the Creator? Or illusory because we exist and act within a complex web of relationships to the rest of Creation? This raises another form of the question: In what sense are our actions "ours"? In what sense are they God's? In what sense are they determined by other factors? Regarding spirituality, a main question has to do with the implications of petitionary prayer for our understanding of the interplay between divine and human action.

I first highlight the obvious—and complex—dynamic between divine sovereignty and human initiative that is evident in our scriptural traditions. Second, I briefly explain the ways subsequent Christian theological tradition has sought to make sense of it. Finally, I outline a contemporary way of negotiation.

Divine Determinism and Invitation for Human Collaboration in Scriptural Testimonies

The dynamic tension reflected in the questions above is well known in both faith traditions' scriptural testimonies. Probably no one else put it as succinctly and pointedly in Christian Scriptures than the Apostle Paul, the main "theologian" of the Christian New Testament: "work out your own salvation with fear and trembling; for it is God who is at work in you, enabling you both to will and to work for his good pleasure" (Phil. 2:12–13). As much as this and similar passages highlight some kind of synergistic or collaborative effort between God and the human person, on the other side, we can easily find passages that seem to be teaching direct divine determinism that could be interpreted to frustrate any genuine notion of human freedom. Just consider this passage from the same apostle's epistle to the Romans:

> "I will have mercy on whom I have mercy, and I will have compassion on whom I have compassion." So it depends not on human will or exertion, but on God who shows mercy. . . . So then he has mercy on whomever he chooses, and he hardens the heart of whomever he chooses. (Rom. 9:15–16, 18)

Similarly, the sage of the Proverbs (16:4) declares: "The LORD has made everything for its purpose, even the wicked for the day of trouble." Or the testimony of the Prophet Isaiah (37:26), speaking of Yahweh's work of destruction: "'Have you not heard that I determined it long ago? I planned from days of old what now I bring to pass. . . .'" And so forth. These and plenty of other passages undoubtedly lean toward divine determinism. That, however, is not the whole picture. Let me briefly seek to balance—and perhaps even further challenge—the matter.

First, there clearly are scriptural passages that endorse and even invite human initiative. Just recall Paul's admonition above for Christians to "work out" their own salvation (Phil. 2:12). Furthermore, countless scriptures command us to pray to God consistently—even "stubbornly," without desire to give up (Luke 11:5–13; 18:1–8). These and many similar passages reveal that even in his sovereignty, the Lord makes his actions in the world contingent—although not ultimately dependent—on human initiative, which of course is possible only when freedom is assumed.

Second, divine sovereignty (or even determinism, if you will) is not that of a despot or tyrant. The assurance of God's omnipotence and omniscience gives robust confidence to the believers, as is repeated over and over again in the testimonies of the Bible: there is no need to worry about the necessities of life, as God is able and willing to care for us (Matt. 6:25–34); there is no reason to give up hope when facing the utmost trials or even death, as God helps us in our "weakness" and knows all things and us better than anyone else (Rom. 8:26–31). Recall also the experience of Joseph, the son of Jacob. Having been forsaken by his brothers and sold as a slave to a foreign land, Joseph testified confidently that "even though you intended to do harm to me, God intended it for good" (Gen. 50:20).

To make sense and negotiate this dynamic diversity in the sacred scriptural tradition, theologians of the past and contemporary times have sought to construct some viable ways of explanation. To those we turn next.

Ways of Negotiation in Christian Tradition[6]

The problem of human freedom in relation to divine sovereignty and foreknowledge occasioned the classical question by the fifth-century opponent of St. Augustine named Evodius, who wondered "how God can have foreknowledge of everything in the future, and yet we do not sin by necessity." Evodius was stuck between a rock and a hard place because "[it] would be an irreligious and completely insane attack on God's foreknowledge to say that something could happen otherwise than as God foreknew."[7] Certainly St. Augustine's strong insistence on divine determinism intensified this dilemma.[8]

For all those who wish to affirm some kind of libertarian form of human freedom (that is, who fear that divine determinism defeats freedom), two key questions emerge, fittingly named the "source question" and "reconciliation question"—that is, respectively, the way God obtains knowledge of the future and the possibility of reconciling the divine foreknowledge and free will.[9] Let me rehearse briefly and critically the classic discussion in Christian tradition.

In many ways the simplest and most commonsense solution to the problem is what can be called—literally—the "simple foreknowledge view." Although it has some contemporary advocates, it is more widely present in tradition. A typical example is the Thomistic view (after the medieval master St. Thomas of Aquinas), which, building on Aristotelian resources, assumes that because God is a simple being (that is, there is no "composition" such as that between essence and existence), it means that God's "act of understanding must be His essence."[10] Since God's knowledge of everything is simple, it means there is no room for contingency (at least ultimately). God's knowledge never changes and, therefore, more or less divine determinism must be assumed. The Augustinian-Calvinistic (after the Protestant Reformer John Calvin) view materially represents this ancient tradition.[11] Should one wish to speak of human freedom, compatibilism seems to be the only option. As to *how* compatibilism is possible, this view does not usually offer any sophisticated explanations.[12]

More appealing intellectually has been the medieval master William of Ockham's "way out"; that is, "there are some truths about the past that do not share in the necessity generally attributed to such truths"—namely, "truths about God's past beliefs [which] are not accidentally necessary."[13] The technical term "accidentally necessary" simply means that the past is "necessary" in the sense of being beyond our control (having taken place[14]).[15] Although the Ockhamist distinction certainly is useful, it seems to me more rhetorical than substantial.[16]

In light of the inadequacies and continuing unresolved problems of the views briefly mentioned above, no wonder new and novel ways of negotiating divine sovereignty and human freedom emerged in Christian theology. The sixteenth-century Roman Catholic (Jesuit) theologian Luis de Molina set out to reconcile two claims long thought to be incompatible: that God is the all-knowing governor of the universe and that individual freedom can prevail only in a universe free of absolute determinism.[17] He came up with a novel concept called "middle knowledge." It holds that God knows, though he has no control over, truths about how any individual would freely choose to act in any situation. Given such knowledge and then creating such a world, God can be truly providential while leaving his creatures genuinely free.[18] Molinism goes further than compatibilism (without leaving behind compatibilist intuitions), which merely holds together divine determinism and human freedom.[19] Molinism seeks to explain *how* God knows the contingent future. To accomplish that, it distinguishes two more forms of divine knowledge: whereas "natural knowledge" is the knowledge of necessary truths (and all logical possibilities) and "free knowledge" encompasses the actual world as it is, "middle knowledge" is the knowledge of the "counterfactuals" of all feasible worlds—that is, what humans might do in any given context. It is best to understand the "moments" in God's knowledge as *logical* rather than temporal moments.[20]

The promise of the Molinist proposal is that it makes it possible to be "an incompatibilist about causal determinism and human freedom (in the relevant sense), but a compatibilist about God's omniscience (foreknowledge) and such freedom."[21] In other words, the libertarian (indeed, strong form of libertarian) interpretation of freedom claims that "the sum total of *God's* activity prior to and at the time of our action cannot determine that action if it is free."[22] On the other hand, as mentioned, Molinism has no desire to compromise the omnipotence and omniscience of God. Briefly put, the "twin pillars" of Molinism are then a belief in the traditional notion of providence (the idea that everything that happens is "specifically" intended or else permitted by God) and libertarianism.[23] Indeed, Molinists go so far as to claim that their view best accounts for the multiplicity of the biblical teaching—although that claim is made by proponents of virtually any other option as well.[24]

Some Concluding Remarks

Space devoted to Molinism already indicates that my own sympathies go with that view. Although I do not consider myself technically a Molinist (any more than I have a desire to defend it as a thought system), and although I do not nec-essarily believe that the dynamic between divine sovereignty and foreknowledge vis-à-vis human freedom can be in any way exhaustively resolved, it seems to me that this view helps us hold in dynamic tension the two biblical convictions pres-ent in scriptures—divine foreknowledge and sovereignty on the one side and human freedom of will on the other side.[25] I am deeply concerned about any reso-lution that might suggest compromising the sovereignty of God, his omnipotence and omniscience. I am also deeply bothered by such accounts of divine determin-ism that appear to make human freedom—and consequently, responsibility—void. Better to aim at humble and modest explanations and be guided by the biblical testimonies which, on the one hand, seem to point in differing directions and yet, on the other hand, speak of the acts and intentions of one and the same God, the Creator of heaven and earth.

Let me put the matter this way: I take the Molinist proposal as heuristic and suggestive. It seems to me that any credible account of the issue has to begin with the acknowledgment of the necessary but not sufficient role of divine foreknowl-edge. Foreknowledge is necessary for God's proper governance (providence) of the world, including foreseeing the future, but not after Augustinian-Calvinist determinism in which God's foreknowledge secures the future by knowing and *determining* his decrees.[26] At the minimum, Molinism goes several steps further than compatibilism in trying to "explain" the reconciliation problem (between divine foreknowledge and human freedom) even if, as expected, it may not be able to offer a total solution.

Something like a Molinist-type explanation is in sync with and funds the foundational biblical conviction of the presence of God in the world through his Spirit. Just consider this one passage from the Old Testament (Ps. 139:7–12):

> [7]Where can I go from your spirit?
> Or where can I flee from your presence?
> [8]If I ascend to heaven, you are there;
> if I make my bed in Sheol, you are there.
> [9]If I take the wings of the morning
> and settle at the farthest limits of the sea,
> [10]even there your hand shall lead me,
> and your right hand shall hold me fast.
> [11]If I say, "Surely the darkness shall cover me,
> and the light around me become night,"
> [12]even the darkness is not dark to you;
> the night is as bright as the day,
> for darkness is as light to you.

If, as Christians believe and confess, the Divine Spirit's universal presence makes possible, permeates, sustains, and guides the life of Creation to which a relative independence has been given graciously by God, then it means that the divine guidance is all-present, all-comprehensive, and all-purposeful—without negating the (relatively speaking) important role of creatures. In such a pneumatological context, the omniscience (full foreknowledge, as it were) of the triune God is understood as the divine omnipresence in Creation, and thus no event or process evades it.[27] That omnipresence, rather than curtailing the freedom—independence—of Creation, constantly makes room for it.

In Christian understanding, freedom is not something that has to be won from God. Freedom is a gracious gift, a hospitable "necessity" (determined by the Creator) for creaturely life to exist. As such it also allows for its misuse, the creature's fleeing away from the Creator or setting one's will against God. Rather than fully determining the choices and life of humans, the omnipresent-omnipotent-omniscient Triune Creator prepares and determines the creaturely environment for such conditions that make possible certain types of free choices but does not determine them, although they are known to God. Even if a person does not freely choose the ideal option(s), the Creator's will is not thereby frustrated, or else only strict determinism follows. The triune God honors the choices of the creatures although those choices never come close to frustrating the eternal divine economy of salvation.

That said, once again, we should be reminded of the need to be modest about a constructive proposal regarding an ancient dilemma. Without being able to solve the problem, perhaps the general framework and some guidelines suggested here may help us better live as responsible persons. Daily immersion in the sacred scriptures in reverent meditation and prayer help us deepen knowledge and spiritual insight as well as, most importantly, cultivate grateful and humble obedience.

Notes

1. I have responded to and defeated these objections to freedom in my *Creation and Humanity*, vol. 3 of *A Constructive Christian Theology for the Pluralistic World* (Grand Rapids, MI: Eerdmans, 2015), chaps. 7 and 13.

2. For the oft-quoted "consequent" statement (that is, what are the consequences if free will is denied) by a premier contemporary defender of free will, see Peter van Inwagen, *An Essay on Free Will* (Oxford: Clarendon, 1983), 16. Much research has been conducted on folk psychology of free will, e.g., E. Nahmias, S. Morris, T. Nadelhoffer, and J. Turner, "Surveying Freedom: Folk Intuitions about Free Will and Moral Responsibility," *Philosophical Psychology* 18, no. 5 (2005): 561–84.

3. Illustrative is the essay seeking to defeat human freedom by neuroscientists Patrick Haggard and Benjamin Libet, "Conscious Intention and Brain Activity," *Journal of Consciousness Studies* 8, no. 1 (2001): 47, which opens with this sentence: "Voluntary action is fundamental to human existence."

4. See, further, Herbert Kane, introduction to *The Oxford Handbook of Free Will*, ed. Herbert Kane, 2nd ed. (Oxford: Oxford University Press, 2011), 3–4.

5. Typically, the question of freedom *from* has dominated philosophical debates, and regretfully the freedom *for* aspect has received much less attention.

6. This section is taken with modifications from my *Creation and Humanity*, chap. 13.

7. Augustine, *On Grace and Free Will* 3.2.

8. On the implications to the doctrine of divine election—a theme also well known in Islamic tradition—see my *Spirit and Salvation*, vol. 4 of *A Constructive Christian Theology for the Pluralistic World* (Grand Rapids, MI: Eerdmans, 2016), chap. 9.

9. As formulated by Alfred J. Freddoso, translator of Luis de Molina, *On Divine Foreknowledge*, Part IV of the *Concordia* (Ithaca, NY: Cornell University Press, 1988), 1. Standard terms used in philosophical accounts of divine sovereignty and human freedom are "compatibilism," according to which determinism can be reconciled with free will, and "incompatibilism," according to which that is not possible. "Libertarianism" is often viewed as a subgroup of incompatibilism, at other times as a virtual synonym.

10. Thomas Aquinas, *Summa Theologica*, 1.14.4.

11. For current advocacy, see David Hunt, "The Simple-Foreknowledge View," in *Divine Foreknowledge: Four Views*, ed. James K. Beilby and Paul R. Eddy (Downers Grove, IL: InterVarsity Press, 2001), 65–103. Martin Luther's *The Bondage of the Will* also materially advocates this view.

12. Cf. Hunt, "Simple-Foreknowledge View," 67. One who sought to provide at least some kind of explanation as to how the simple foreknowledge view might work is the sixth-century philosopher Boethius with his "eternity solution": because God is timeless ("eternal" in this specific understanding), the question of who/what decided certain events in a particular human being's life does not arise; there is no interval between, say, t_1 and t_2 (t = moment of time). Apart from the difficulty with that concept of time (and eternity), there are other difficulties, both theological (for example, concerning the possi-

bility of God's action in time/history) and logical (the confusion of "conditional" and "natural" necessity in relation to divine foreknowledge). See Greg Rich, "Boethius on Divine Foreknowledge and Human Free Will," *Thinking about Religion* 5 (2005): n.p, http://organizations.uncfsu.edu/ncrsa/journal/v05/rich_boethius.htm. Nor do I see much promise in the eighteenth-century American theologian Jonathan Edwards's argument in his 1754 *Freedom of the Will* (p. 123) that, notwithstanding ironclad divine determinism and, as a result, total rejection of all forms of libertarianism, God's foreknowledge per se does not determine events, because everything simply happens as it happens, whether God foreknows it or not. While that may be true rhetorically, I don't see how it could bring any more consolation than strict compatibilism.

13. William Hasker, "Divine Knowledge and Human Freedom," in *The Oxford Handbook of Free Will*, 2nd ed., ed. Herbert Kane (Oxford: Oxford University Press, 2011), 44. A contemporary advocate of Ockham's solution is Marilyn McCord Adams, "Is the Existence of God a 'Hard' Fact?," *Philosophical Review* 76, no. 4 (1967): 492–503.

14. Consider this example: Having turned down an offer for a full scholarship from a prestigious college so that it goes to another interested person, the student "must" work while in school (or have a rich uncle) in order to finance it. It is only after the refusal to receive that this "accidental" event (at least for the next academic year) is "necessarily" ruled out (although in itself the event is not necessary).

15. For a current important discussion, see Alvin Plantinga, "On Ockham's Way Out," *Faith and Philosophy* 3, no. 3 (1986): 235–69.

16. For a state-of-the-art conclusion (that none of these options above has won wide support), see Hasker, "Divine Knowledge," 49.

17. For leading current Molinist philosophical accounts, see Thomas P. Flint, *Divine Providence: The Molinist Account* (Ithaca, NY: Cornell University Press, 1998); and William Lane Craig, *The Only Wise God* (Eugene, OR: Wipf & Stock, 1999).

18. See Kenneth Perszyk, introduction to *Molinism: The Contemporary Debate*, ed. Ken Perszyk (New York: Oxford University Press, 2011), 4–5. An accurate, nontechnical introduction to Molinism is William Lane Craig, "The Middle Knowledge View," in *Divine Foreknowledge: Four Views*, ed. James K. Beilby and Paul R. Eddy (Downers Grove, IL: InterVarsity Press, 2001), 119–43.

19. See John Martin Fischer, "Putting Molinism in Its Place," in *Molinism: The Contemporary Debate*, ed. Ken Perszyk (New York: Oxford University Press, 2011), 209.

20. Craig, *The Only Wise God*, 127.

21. Fischer, "Putting Molinism in Its Place," 209 (not Fischer's own opinion).

22. Perszyk, introduction, 4.

23. The standard account is Flint, *Divine Providence*.

24. One of the Old Testament passages that highlights the Molinist "middle knowledge" is an incident from the life of the first king of Israel, Saul (1 Sam. 23:1–14). Saul, chasing David (later the second king and God-appointed successor to Saul) in an attempt to kill him, is told that David can be found in a city where the capture is possible. David inquires about the Lord's will by consulting a priest's "ephod," a device to give a simple "yes" or "no" answer to a question. The divine response—namely, that David would be killed by the people of Keilah—does not come to pass, because David chooses not to stay in Keilah. This is supposed to evince not only God's "simple" but also "middle knowledge" as he knows what would happen under both circumstances (whether David decided to stay or leave the fatal city). Other favorite Molinist passages include Proverbs 4:11: "I

have taught you the way of wisdom; I have led you in the paths of uprightness," which is also supposed to show evidence of the divine middle knowledge and full human cooperation. The New Testament choice passages includes Jesus's harsh words of judgment in Matthew 11:23 ("And you, Capernaum, will you be exalted to heaven? No, you will be brought down to Hades. For if the deeds of power done in you had been done in Sodom, it would have remained until this day"), which can be interpreted as saying that the people of Sodom (destroyed by God because of godlessness) had circumstances perfectly fixed for them, but even then God knew what their response was (that is, lack of repentance) and acted accordingly. For details, see Craig, "Middle Knowledge View," 123–25.

25. A highly useful, succinct account of standard objections can be found in John D. Laing, "Middle Knowledge," *Internet Encyclopedia of Philosophy: A Peer-Reviewed Academic Resource*, June 27, 2005, http://www.iep.utm.edu/middlekn/. In my mind, the most serious potential objection to Molinism has to do with counterfactuals, the so-called grounding objection; that is, counterfactuals seem not to be based on any categorical facts about the world. Behind the objection is the long-term debate about whether "truth makers" are needed to make a statement true—that is, its truth-claim needs a reference to another "fact" or "state of affairs" (Bernard Russell; J. L. Austin)—or whether "truth supervenes on being," meaning that any two possible worlds alike with respect to what exists and what properties are exemplified are alike with respect to what is true (see David Lewis, "Truthmaking and Difference-Making," *Noûs* 35, no. 4 [2001]: 602–15). While I leave this complicated and thorny question to be debated by expert philosophers, I can't help but be persuaded by the commonsense objection of the noted contemporary Christian philosopher A. Plantinga: "It seems to me much clearer that some counterfactuals of freedom are at least possibly true than that the truth of propositions must, in general, be founded in this way." See Plantinga, "Reply to Robert M. Adams," in *Alvin Plantinga*, ed. James E. Tomberlin and Peter van Inwagen (Dordrecht: Reidel, 1985), 374.

26. See Perszyk, *Molinism: The Contemporary Debate*.

27. As detailed in my *Trinity and Revelation*, vol. 2 of *A Constructive Christian Theology for the Pluralistic World* (Grand Rapids, MI: Eerdmans, 2014), chap. 12.

Scripture Dialogue 3

Human Action within the Sovereignty of God

Passages from the Qur'ān[1]

Group A

Al-A'rāf (7):172

And when your Lord took from the Children of Adam, from their loins, their seed and made them bear witness over themselves, [asking them,] "Am I not your Lord?" They said, "Yea, indeed we do so bear witness"; lest you should say on the Day of Resurrection, "Indeed of this we were unaware."

Yūnus (10):19

Humankind were but a single community, but then differed. And were it not for a [decreed] word that had already preceded from your Lord, it would have been decided between them regarding that over which they differed.

Al-Isrā' (17):84

Everyone acts according to his [particular] character (*shakila*).

Āl 'Imrān (3):193

Our Lord, we have indeed heard a caller calling to belief, saying, "Believe in your Lord!" And so we believed. Our Lord, forgive us then our sins and absolve us of our evil deeds, and receive us [at death] with the pious.

Al-Ra'd (13):11

He has trailing angels, to his front and his rear, guarding him by God's command. Truly God does not change the lot of a people, unless they change what is in their souls. And if God should will misfortune for a people, there is nothing that can avert it, and they have no protectors apart from Him.

Group B

Al-Tawba (9):94

And God will see your work, and [so will] His messenger, then you will be returned to the Knower of the unseen and the visible, and He will inform you of what you used to do.[2]

Al-Ṣāffāt (37):61

For the like of this [reward] let [all] those who [are given to] work, work.

Al-Muddaththir (74):32–47

[32]No Indeed! By the moon! [33]By the night when it recedes! [34]By the dawn when it brightens! [35]Indeed it is one of the greatest [signs]—[36]a warner to humankind, [37]to those of you who wish to advance or linger behind. [38]Every soul is hostage to what it has earned, [39]except the people of the right hand, [40][who will be] in gardens, [41]wondering about the guilty: [42]"What path led you into Hell?" [43]They [will] answer, "We were not of those who performed the prayer, [44]nor did we feed the poor, [45]but used to gossip with the gossipers [46]and used to deny the Day of Judgement, [47]until [finally] the Certainty came to us."

Luqmān (31):20

Do you not see that God has disposed for you all that is in the heavens and all that is in the earth and He has showered upon you His graces, the outward and the inward?

Group C

Al-Fajr (89):14–16

[14]Assuredly your Lord is ever on the watch; [15]as for man, whenever his Lord tests Him and is generous towards him with [His] graces, he says, "My Lord has been

generous to me"; [16]but when He tests him and constricts for him his provision, he says, "My Lord has humiliated me."

Āl ʿImrān (3):103

Safeguard yourselves by [clinging to] God's rope, all together, and do not become divided; remember God's grace upon you when you were enemies, and He composed your hearts so that by His grace you became brothers; and you were upon the brink of a pit of fire; but He delivered you from it. Thus God makes clear to you His signs so that you may be guided.

Al-Raʿd (13):26

God expands provision for whomever He wishes, and constricts [it for whomever He wishes]. They exult in the life of this world, but the life of this world compared to the Hereafter is but [a trifling] enjoyment.

Al-Raʿd (13):38–39

[38]. . . or every term, there is a book. [39]God effaces and confirms whatever He wishes and with Him is the Mother of the Book.

Al-Ḥijr (15):21

And there is not a thing but that the stores thereof are with Us, and We do not send it down except in a known measure.

Al-Shūrā (42):27

For were God to expand His provision to [all of] His servants, they would surely become covetous in the earth; but He sends down in the measure that He wishes.

Al-Ṭalāq (65):2–3, 7

[2]. . . And whoever is wary of God, He will make a way out for him [3]and provide for him whence he does not reckon. And whoever puts his trust in God, He will suffice him. Indeed God fulfils His command. Verily God has set a measure for

everything. . . . [7]Let the affluent man expend out of his affluence. And let he whose provision has been straitened for him, expend of what God has given him. God does not charge any soul except [according to] what He has given it. God will bring about ease after hardship.

Yūnus (10):11

And if God were to hasten for humankind the evil [consequence of their actions] as they are wont to hasten the good, their term [of life] would long since have been concluded.

Passages from the Bible

Genesis 50:19–20

[19]But Joseph said to them, "Do not be afraid! Am I in the place of God? [20]Even though you intended to do harm to me, God intended it for good, in order to preserve a numerous people, as he is doing today."

Proverbs 3:5–7

[5]Trust in the Lord with all your heart,
and do not rely on your own insight.
[6]In all your ways acknowledge him,
and he will make straight your paths.
[7]Do not be wise in your own eyes;
fear the Lord, and turn away from evil.

Proverbs 16:1–4

[1]The plans of the mind belong to mortals,
but the answer of the tongue is from the Lord.
[2]All one's ways may be pure in one's own eyes,
but the Lord weighs the spirit.
[3]Commit your work to the Lord,
and your plans will be established.
[4]The Lord has made everything for its purpose,
even the wicked for the day of trouble.

Isaiah 37:23–27

[23]"Whom have you mocked and reviled?
Against whom have you raised your voice
and haughtily lifted your eyes?
Against the Holy One of Israel!
[23]By your servants you have mocked the Lord,
and you have said, "With my many chariots
I have gone up the heights of the mountains,
to the far recesses of Lebanon;
I felled its tallest cedars,
its choicest cypresses;
I came to its remotest height,
its densest forest.
[24]I dug wells
and drank waters,
I dried up with the sole of my foot
all the streams of Egypt."
[25]"Have you not heard
that I determined it long ago?
I planned from days of old
what now I bring to pass,
that you should make fortified cities
crash into heaps of ruins,
[26]while their inhabitants, shorn of strength,
are dismayed and confounded;
they have become like plants of the field
and like tender grass,
like grass on the housetops,
blighted before it is grown.
[27]"I know your rising up and your sitting down,
your going out and coming in,
and your raging against me."

Matthew 6:25–34

[25]"Therefore I tell you, do not worry about your life, what you will eat or what you will drink, or about your body, what you will wear. Is not life more than food, and the body more than clothing? [26]Look at the birds of the air; they neither sow nor reap nor gather into barns, and yet your heavenly Father feeds them. Are you not of more value than they? [27]And can any of you by worrying add a single hour

to your span of life? [28]And why do you worry about clothing? Consider the lilies of the field, how they grow; they neither toil nor spin, [29]yet I tell you, even Solomon in all his glory was not clothed like one of these. [30]But if God so clothes the grass of the field, which is alive today and tomorrow is thrown into the oven, will he not much more clothe you—you of little faith? [31]Therefore do not worry, saying, 'What will we eat?' or 'What will we drink?' or 'What will we wear?' [32]For it is the Gentiles who strive for all these things; and indeed your heavenly Father knows that you need all these things. [33]But strive first for the kingdom of God and his righteousness, and all these things will be given to you as well.

[34]"So do not worry about tomorrow, for tomorrow will bring worries of its own. Today's trouble is enough for today."

Luke 11:5–13

[5]And he said to them, "Suppose one of you has a friend, and you go to him at midnight and say to him, 'Friend, lend me three loaves of bread; [6]for a friend of mine has arrived, and I have nothing to set before him.' [7]And he answers from within, 'Do not bother me; the door has already been locked, and my children are with me in bed; I cannot get up and give you anything.' [8]I tell you, even though he will not get up and give him anything because he is his friend, at least because of his persistence he will get up and give him whatever he needs.

[9]"So I say to you, Ask, and it will be given to you; search, and you will find; knock, and the door will be opened for you. [10]For everyone who asks receives, and everyone who searches finds, and for everyone who knocks, the door will be opened. [11]Is there anyone among you who, if your child asks for a fish, will give a snake instead of a fish? [12]Or if the child asks for an egg, will give a scorpion? [13]If you then, who are evil, know how to give good gifts to your children, how much more will the heavenly Father give the Holy Spirit to those who ask him!"

Romans 8:28–31

[28]We know that all things work together for good for those who love God, who are called according to his purpose. [29]For those whom he foreknew he also predestined to be conformed to the image of his Son, in order that he might be the firstborn within a large family. [30]And those whom he predestined he also called; and those whom he called he also justified; and those whom he justified he also glorified. [31]What then are we to say about these things? If God is for us, who is against us?

Philippians 2:12–13

[12]Therefore, my beloved, just as you have always obeyed me, not only in my presence, but much more now in my absence, work out your own salvation with fear and trembling; [13]for it is God who is at work in you, enabling you both to will and to work for his good pleasure.

Notes

1. Translation by Feras Hamza.
2. Al-Tawba (9):105 reads identically.

PART V

Reflection

Discussion in Doha

Listening in on the Building Bridges Process

LUCINDA MOSHER

GEORGETOWN UNIVERSITY'S SCHOOL of Foreign Service in Qatar (SFS-Q) provides a congenial atmosphere for appreciative conversation—the sort of frank and spirited exchange at the core of the Building Bridges Seminar. In 2015 SFS-Q provided us a spacious lounge with comfortable furniture and ample space for buffet-style meals, an adjacent meeting room large enough for closed lectures and plenary discussions to take place "in the round," and, nearby, a small classroom for each of our four dialogue groups. It is in these predetermined groups, balanced by religion and gender as best as can be, that the main work of the seminar takes place. These groups remain constant throughout the seminar. Each has a moderator whose primary task is to ensure that everyone can and does participate in the discussion.

Each seminar member is provided, and is encouraged to study in advance, a booklet of texts (from the Bible and the Qur'ān, primarily) chosen for their relevance to the meeting's subthemes—which, for 2015, were God's creation and its goal, the dignity and task of humankind, and human action within the sovereignty of God. The small group process begins by opening this booklet to the texts appointed for that session. Each group member points out a phrase (or even a single word) that has caught his or her attention, perhaps mentioning a question it raised. This practice, which defers discussion until each person has had the opportunity to speak, allows interpenetrating themes to emerge. Typically, the resulting conversations are deep, multidirectional, and may—like labyrinths—double back on themselves. Since the 2015 study booklet included a larger number of scripture passages than had been usual in previous years, conversations for each session were more varied in their focus from one group to the next than had been typical in other years. Nevertheless, eight topics—God's act of creation; the creation of humanity "in God's image"; vicegerency, trust, and covenant; creation's purpose as worship of God; sin; humanity's task; creation and creativity;

and predeterminism, free will, foreknowledge, and theodicy—were given attention by every group. Here are some highlights.[1]

God's Act of Creation

The Genesis 1 account of divine Creation over the course of seven days was
discussed from a variety of perspectives. One Christian turned his group's attention to the fact that the Genesis Creation narrative is characterized by a refrain:
at each step of the way, things are "good" or "very good"; God's relation to Creation is one of joy. That emphasis on joy and rejoicing reminded one of the Muslims of partying. A Christian affirmed that images of a party or banquet are
found in both testaments, and that the New Testament speaks of "joy in heaven."
Another group brought the Genesis passage into conversation with Sūra al-Raʿd
(13):2–4, which begins, "It is God who raised up the heavens with no visible
supports and then established Himself on the throne; He has subjected the sun
and the moon each to pursue its course for an appointed time; He regulates all
things, and makes the revelations clear so that you may be certain of meeting
your Lord." One Muslim noted a sense here and elsewhere in the Qurʾān that two
things are happening at once: "On the one hand, the Qurʾān teaches that the world
is created *for* human beings. It's anthropocentric. But, on the other hand, according to the Qurʾān, there are things in nature we humans *can't* understand." Similarly, a Christian called his group's attention to Yūnus (10):5. "In this verse, God
explains his signs," he noted, "not to everyone, but to those who are *predisposed
to understand.* Christians also would recall that Jesus says, 'Those who have ears
to hear. . . .'" A Muslim nodded: "Seeds fall on the ground—and it depends on
the ground. Some seeds will sprout; some seeds will be useless." Some people
simply are not prepared, another Muslim suggested. Another Christian concurred. "Discernment is necessary. Many people will not 'get' the signs; wisdom
requires eyes to see."

Creation of Humanity "in God's Image"

Turning to God's creation of humanity, one participant noted how often the Creation imagery of both scriptures speaks of humanity's having come "from
dust"—from unpleasant stuff. Perhaps this is a reminder, this scholar mused, that
we are to remember our "place." One group took note of al-Anbiyāʾ (21):30, "We
made everything from water," then turned to al-Muʾminūn (23):12, "We created
man from an essence of clay, then We placed him as a drop of fluid in a safe
place. . . ." Referring to this latter verse, a Christian wondered, "How did Arabs
in the Qurʾān's original audience hear this passage? How do contemporary Muslims hear it?" A Muslim responded that it is heard in a biological sense: "the

scientific aspect of the Qur'ān is what drew me into Islam. It brought all my science lessons to life." Regarding the biblical account of God's Creation of humanity, a Muslim found it interesting that what God decides to make in his image is not a mountain or water; rather, it is humankind. In response to questions about humanity having been made in God's image and after God's likeness (Gen. 1:26), one group gave considerable time to study of the Hebrew vocabulary expressing this idea.

Responding to concerns about the very notion of the "image of God," one Christian explained that the Genesis text does not say that the human *is* the image of God; rather the human is created *in* God's image, *after* God's likeness. "It may be helpful to know that, in ancient times, boundaries of dominion were marked by images of the king," he explained. "God's boundaries are marked by his 'images' (i.e., humans). It may also be helpful to remember that a portrait is utterly incomparable, yet it is a 'likeness.'" In fact, Genesis 1 and 2 have to do with God's provision for all Creation; humans are simply part of this comprehensive economy. Some Muslim participants were interested in hearing more about the relationship between the Christian doctrine of humanity as made in God's image and Christian understandings of immanence and transcendence—which led invariably into rousing discussions of the Christian doctrine of the Incarnation.[2]

Returning more specifically to the topic of the structure of Creation, a Muslim observed that, according to Genesis 2:15, there's "work" in Eden. A Christian concurred, explaining that initially Edenic work was pleasurable, becoming burdensome only after the Fall. According to Genesis 2:15, another Christian added, "work is a good gift of God—which is a beautiful notion, a beautiful image. Now, for so many people—given the need for income—work is a curse; work is ambivalent."

Vicegerency, Trust, and Covenant

Much time was spent in consideration of *khalīfa* (a Qur'ānic term often translated as "vicegerent" or "successor"), the linguistically related term *khilāfa* (having to do with the concept or institution of vicegerency and caliphate but also the notion of stewardship), and *amāna* (often translated as "trust"). Several Muslims noted that *khilāfa* and *amāna* name closely related concepts and are seen as synonyms by some.

One Muslim called attention to the notion set forth by Ibn al-'Arabī that all humans have the potential to internalize the Divine Names and to mirror or reflect them totally, thus to merit the title *khalīfa*. The thought that the whole of humanity is God's vicegerent is quite empowering, another Muslim agreed. However, she pointed out, it is important to differentiate between the mystical notion of *khilāfa* as mirror of the divine attributes and the political understanding of *khalīfa* as ruler. The notion of *khilāfa* can be hijacked by dictators, one participant stressed;

the question of who can claim *khilāfa* legitimately is of utmost importance. As another Muslim made clear, the notion of *khilāfa* has never been static. "The first successors of the Prophet resisted the label of Khalīfat Allah, considering it too big a burden," he explained. "Instead, they'd say, 'Call me the Successor of the Prophet of God.'" Only over time did the term take on the sense of king, sultan, or "emperor as 'shadow of God on earth.'" In fact, another Muslim insisted, "*khalīfa* as vicegerent" as having to do with power and dominion is a modern notion. After some discussion, his colleagues concurred that, according to Islam, humanity has a role *within* Creation, not *over* Creation. From an Islamic point of view, one Muslim clarified, humans are a "middle creature," always defined from two directions: simultaneously having some authority, thus ennobled; and totally under God, thus meant to be completely subservient.

Turning to Genesis 1:28, one Muslim underscored the word "dominion" in the translation, commenting that the original Hebrew word is far more neutral than its English equivalent. This passage has had implications both for environmentalists and for people advocating for empire. It can be used to exploit. However, the original Hebrew term supports a notion of "responsibility." The group agreed that, as is so often the case with scripture, this verse yields multiple interpretations and thus has multiple real-world implications. Continuing in this vein, several Muslims asserted that Qur'ānic notions of *amāna* (trust) and *khilāfa* (vicegerency, stewardship) are more sociopolitical than environmental. The question of whether (thus, where) the Qur'ān gives guidance on environmentalism provoked intense discussion in one group, with some Muslims making a case for environmentalism based on the Qur'ān and others disagreeing. Pointing to al-Aḥzāb (33):72, "Truly We offered the Trust unto the heavens and the earth and the mountains," a Muslim underscored this verse's importance for Sufism, Islamic philosophy, and *kalām* (theology): "There is extensive discussion of *amāna* in Islamic literature," he said; "we might say that the Trust of God is the Spirit of God."

Responding to Muslim questions about the biblical notion of "covenant," a Christian defined it as an agreement initiated by God. In the Noachic Covenant, he explained, God pledges faithfulness to all of humanity and invites humanity to loving obedience. This is followed by the Abrahamic Covenant and the Mosaic Covenant. The first covenant, with Noah, has no conditions; neither does the covenant with Abraham. The covenant with Moses is conditional, and the people broke it—a theme of the Old Testament books of the Prophets. Finally, there is the New Covenant in Jesus. "In Colossians, we read of God reconciling all things to God's self through Christ. Christ as covenant means that the covenant absolutely includes everyone; it is for the sake of the whole world."

A Christian wanted to know whether the trust is like the covenant. "God seems to have offered the trust foolishly; humankind was foolish to accept. But what exactly was offered?" Her group readily took up this question, with one Muslim explaining the notion of a primordial covenant. "The Qur'ān tells us that everything returns to God; even animals have a resurrection." Another Muslim interjected: "*Amāna* has to do with the relationship between humankind and the world, between humanity and Creation." The first Muslim continued, saying that, in Islamic understanding, "The Bible's Noachic Covenant comes close to the terms of the Qur'ānic primordial covenant. The primordial covenant was made with disembodied souls. It was a covenant made *outside* history from a human point of view. This is unique to the Qur'ānic account of history." Indeed, another Muslim noted, both the Qur'ān and the Ḥadīth refer in some places to "things that are outside of history—some that are prehistory, some posthistory. What, after all, is a *day* with God? It is outside of time."

Creation's Purpose as Worship of God

For a ready answer to the question of the purpose of Creation, someone pointed particularly to al-Dhāriyāt (51):56, in which God says, "I have created man and jinn for no reason except for my worship." The first step, he explained, is recognition—acknowledgment with the intellect and the heart, that there *is* a creator. Without such recognition, there is no worship. Having noted that human beings have been created to worship God, discussion focused on the root and reference of the Arabic term *'ibāda*. One group noted that *'ibāda*, usually translated as "worship," comes from the same root as *'abd* (servant)—which comes through in Ibn Taymiyya's definition of *'ibāda* as "everything we do that maintains relationship with God." While indeed the triliteral root at play here produces the words for "slave," "servant," and "subject," another group noted that it also has to do with knowledge—particularly, knowing God. Thus, there are linguistic connections between worship of God and the dignity and empowering rather than the demeaning of the human being. One Christian noted how her group had reflected upon God's purpose in creating the world as "directed to worship and gratitude—to attitudes rather than actions—to which God responds." That is, creation's purpose is relational: "it reflects, it shows forth, the beauty of God and the Divine Names—including their abundant juxtaposition."

One group brought 1 John 3:1–3 (which begins, "See what love the Father has given us, that we should be called children of God; and that is what we are . . .") into conversation with al-Naḥl (16):13–17 (which begins, "He has made of benefit to you the many-coloured things He has multiplied on the earth. There truly are signs in this for those who take it to heart"). Remarking that the passage from 1 John speaks of love poured out, one of the Christians asserted that it "is about our intimacy with God; about knowing and being known, in the context of *love*. We are the beloved: we are God's children *now*. This passage is about hope, but also delight. It uses finite language for the infinite." Someone else noted that the passage from Al-Naḥl says to "reflect" and to "remember" as both capacity and charge to "know" (thus to worship) God. The group observed the interesting link between remembrance and reflection, on the one hand, and gratitude, praise, and the human need to be guided, on the other.

The language of Psalms 8 and 104—both of which give voice to human praise of God's glory—caused a Muslim to ask, "In Christian theology and faith, what *is* glory? Wonder? Divine beauty? Holiness? Is it the fullness of God?" Suggesting that his group look at Colossians 1:19, which mentions God's "fullness," a Christian explained: "Glory belongs to God but invokes awe and wonder in us; it belongs to God but is transferred to human beings (as we read in Psalm 8) and to children of God (according to Romans 8)." Indeed, said another Christian, "it is strange that we 'give glory to God!' What an amazing thing in itself! And an amazing thing to respond to; and an amazing thing to share in and to receive from God."

Much discussion of the economy of supplication emerged, provoked by the seminar's subtheme of human action within God's sovereignty. One participant observed that al-Baqara (2):186—"I am near. I answer the call of the caller . . ."— is a verse given by God in response to the Muslim community asking the Prophet Muhammad how they should go about getting God's attention. Concurring, another Muslim described the purpose of *dhikr* (remembrance of God) as theurgic, in that it "brings God alive" for the worshipper. "Repetition is how a child learns. You repeat to actualize. 'To remember' and 'to mention' are two meanings of the same Arabic word." A Christian saw a connection here to the Eastern Orthodox liturgical practice of saying Kyrie Eleison forty times and reiteration of "Remember him in eternal life."

One Christian noted that Jesus himself was a man of prayer. In addition to Jesus's instruction to his disciples on how to pray (in which he gives the template often called "the Lord's Prayer"), she had in mind the lengthy prayer of Jesus recorded in John 17 (Jesus's "High Priestly Prayer") and the many Gospel references to Jesus's withdrawing to a solitary place to pray (such as Matt. 14:23 and 26:36–44; Mark 1:35; Luke 5:16; 6:12; 9:16; 11:1; and 22:41–43). Furthermore, she added, the New Testament contains many admonitions to pray without ceasing. Prayer is powerful, she asserted. Human beings have the need and the instinct to ask, another Christian observed, noting that the parables in Luke 11 (which the seminar was studying) are about the place of supplication in bringing about God's will. "God's goodness is not dependent on our asking; but our asking may speed God up!" A third Christian offered a different perspective: "God's giving is all there already." The second Christian responded. "It is not that God is withholding till we ask; it is that we are not ready to receive until we ask!"

Noting the theme of persistence in the Luke 11 parables, a Muslim mentioned the Sufi teaching that when one knocks on the door of a *shaykh*, one should expect that the door will be slammed in one's face; but one should knock again! Expanding on this, another Muslim pointed out that, according to the Ḥadīth, a prayer can be answered in any of several ways: (1) you can receive exactly what you asked for; (2) you can receive almost what you asked for; or (3) God saves up all of his answers for Paradise—and you receive God's response to your prayer there. In response, this group turned to Matthew 6:25–34, entering into a close reading of the passage in which Jesus says, "do not worry about your life. . . . Look at the birds of the air; they neither sow nor reap nor gather into barns, and yet your heavenly Father feeds them. Are you not of more value than they?"

Sin, Fall, and Belief

Consideration of the goal of God's creation led one group into a difficult but rich discussion of sin, including the nature of the Fall and its place in Christian theology and understanding. Among their questions was whether the Fall practically obliterates the "goodness" of Creation, in light of God's declaring (in Genesis 1) that Creation *is* very good, and ways in which the notion of the goodness of Creation persists biblically, especially in the Psalms. "Christians may think of Adam and Fall, not in historical terms, but in evolutionary terms," one noted, citing the Orthodox theologian Alexander Men. "Romans 5 speaks of Adam, and Christ as Second Adam," another Christian explained. "Adam represents all of humankind. The notion of a representative figure comes very early in scripture."

Discussion of Christian understandings of the Fall was driven in part by Muslim questions raised by the Bible's inclusion of two distinct Creation accounts in Genesis (chapters 1 and 2). One Christian pointed out that "as Christians, we can't choose to ignore one of them. We've been given both accounts, both are true, and we have to live with both. We have to read scripture in community; and many of us don't want to be limited to one textual commentary." Particularly in responding to Muslim questions about the Genesis account of the creation of woman (2:18), several Christians asserted the contribution of feminist exegesis.

Having listened to the story of the temptation of Adam and Eve in Genesis 3:1–13, one Muslim noted with surprise that Satan was not mentioned. Indeed, in the Genesis account, the pivotal character is a serpent—a wild animal. "The serpent says to the woman, 'You'll get knowledge . . . ,'" a Muslim observed. "The serpent speaks his own truth," answered one of the Christians; "you will 'know' means you will 'experience.' Here, 'knowing' does not mean 'rationality.'" Another Christian described the Genesis account of the "Fall" as a beautiful reminder that

> humans live in tension. They are creatures, like the rest of creation; but they are creative: "like" God, but not like God. Humans are the only such creatures. In this tension and difficulty, we find we want *not* to be creatures, but rather wish to become "just like" God (which in fact is only one part of who we are). This is part of the theme of mediation: using our creativity within the *givenness* of creation. We want to know, to determine, "good and evil"—just like, but precisely

apart from, God. We humans may see God as a competitor! We express this as rebellion, rejection, idolatry.

A third Christian continued, "The serpent uses truths to deceive! Sin and evil do not (only) 'begin' in the human heart: part of their mystery is their externality and (pseudo-) attraction."

A Muslim noted that, in the Qur'ānic account of the events in the primordial garden, a fundamental difference is established between Iblis's disobedience and the disobedience of Adam and Eve. According to the Qur'ān, there is "a failure" with consequences, not unlike a biblical account—but without rupture of human nature. The Qur'ānic notion is that this failure does not require redemption. Rather, from a Qur'ānic point of view, someone explained, Iblis misleads Adam and makes him forget his internal capacity to know and worship God. Adam's lapse is his forsaking the better option. This is not *sin*, however. Adam is a prophet, so (according to Islamic doctrine) he cannot sin.

A Muslim asked for clarification of Genesis 1:28: "God blessed them, and God said to them, 'Be fruitful and multiply, and fill the earth and subdue it; and have dominion over the fish of the sea and over the birds of the air and over every living thing that moves upon the earth.'" Specifically, he wanted help in understanding the use of the term "subdue" in this verse: how does it relate to current ethical and environmental concerns? This brought the conversation back to understandings of humanity as having been made in God's image. As one Christian put it, in order to be *like* God—something that Christians are called to be—Christians look to Christ to understand *what* the image is *like*. They discover that they are to "be like" self-sacrificial love. By extension, humanity is to treat the world as Christ does—not as rapacious rulers would. In response, one Muslim expressed her appreciation of the poetic nature of Colossians 1:15–17: "[Christ] is the image of the invisible God, the firstborn of all creation; for in him all things in heaven and on earth were created, things visible and invisible, whether thrones or dominions or rulers or powers—all things have been created through him and for him. He himself is before all things, and in him all things hold together." She wondered whether this biblical passage had to do with vicegerency. While acknowledging that it could be read in that way, a Christian participant suggested that Chrisitan readings of this text are likely to emphasize God's eternal word experienced in Jesus in the language of flesh and blood.

Humanity's Task

When a Muslim asked what, from a Christian point of view, is the task of humankind, one responded that it is to wait in trustful hope for the coming of God's *basileia* (kingdom). *Basileia*—righteous rule—is at the center of Jesus's teaching, she explained. For example, when, in the Lord's Prayer, Christians are taught to say, "let your kingdom come," they are in fact saying, "let your *basilea* come."

Someone explained that *basileia* is bigger than "Church"; all are included in God's *basileia*. "The fact that the Kingdom is broader than the Church is at the heart of why we should be involved in positive interfaith relations." In contrast to the *basileia*, the Church is kenotic, said another Christian. The role of the Church is to pour itself out for all; it does not exist for itself. Following up, a Muslim asked whether the Church is to be seen as a force for making the world sacred. "The Church is a force for celebrating the sacredness of an already sacred world," a Christian responded.

As discussion of the task of humankind came to a close, a Christian observed that thinking about what the two traditions teach about the dignity and the ambiguity of humankind is not simple:

> I am struck by the ways in which what we are *able to do*—our capacity, our dignity—and what we are *called to do*—our task, our vocation—always involve a close interlinking of (1) worship, praise, and prayer (heart/spirit) (2) *with* justice, mercy, good acts (will/body), *and with* (3) reflections and thinking (mind/intellect)—such that these are different but not separate, always interwoven, always linked. And so our dignity and vocation seem *simple*: we *just* have to worship God, seek truth, and act well; but in fact, they are complex, with these interwoven aspects.

Creation versus Creativity

Regarding the language of *creativity*, a Christian asked whether there is an Islamic notion of human creativity as participation in divine creativity. One Muslim responded that humans are the most complete theophany. "They embody God's attributes. So they create!" The Qur'ān says that God is the Best of Creators, another Muslim noted; in some Islamic traditions, humans can indeed be cocreators with God. The term *khaliq* (creator) can indeed be used of "*other than God.*" Continuing this theme of nuances of vocabulary, a Christian offered an interesting perspective: "When we study the history of English vocabulary, we find that no one talked about 'creativity' before the nineteenth century. It implies the originality of the artist. It implies the artist creating out of nothing. So, we must be careful how we use it. Before the nineteenth century, it was more normal to talk simply of 'craftsmanship.'"

Predeterminism and Free Will, Foreknowledge, and Theodicy

Closely related to understandings of God as Creator are matters related to God's sovereignty, thus notions of divine predeterminism versus human free will. A participant noted that, among Christians, "there are two streams of thought on this notion: the first is that everything that God knows, God determines; the second is that, whatever are the options, God knows—without determining exactly what we'll choose." The second of these modes has lots of currency in popular Islamic thought, one Muslim responded.

"All language about God's foreknowledge is metaphorical," one Christian asserted. Referring to Isaiah 37:28 ("I know your rising up and your sitting down, your going out and coming in, and your raging against me"), he argued that "God knows perfectly well—as a parent knows what a child is up to. This is 'knowing'—not as orchestrating the actions of an automaton, but as being incredibly personal and close. 'Knowing' is not oppressive." One Muslim noted that within the Ash'arite tradition, there is a distinction between knowledge and power as two separate attributes of God. This led in turn to a discussion of the place of paradox in theology.

One group dug deeply into Sūra Yūnus (10):19, which reads: "All people were originally a single community, but later they differed. If it had not been for a word from your Lord, the preordained judgement would already have been passed between them regarding their differences." The verse caused them to puzzle over the extent to which human diversity is original, God-given blessing, versus the extent to which it is the result of disobedience; and whether differences are the *result* or *cause* of conflict.

Consideration of the relationship between God's foreknowledge and human action always raises the problem of theodicy. That is, if God is all-knowing, all-powerful, and all-loving, why does God allow "sin?" Why does God not stop "evil?" Relatedly, why is suffering in nature outside of what is caused by humans? A Muslim noted that, in back-to-back passages, the Qur'ān says that (1) Everything *good* comes from God; bad comes from you; and (2) *Everything* comes from God! What is *bad* is *testing*. Another Muslim added: "The Qur'ān says that something you dislike may be good for you; something you like may be bad for you. Something that seems bad now may later prove to be better." The first Muslim nodded, adding: "an early Islamic creed said that what hit you could not have missed you; what missed you could not have hit you." Reflecting on this exchange, one Muslim asserted that considering the problem of evil is a different matter from considering the problem of *sin*.

During a discussion of al-A'rāf (7):172—in which God asks human beings "Am I not your Lord?"—one Christian noted that the English word *Lord* actually comes from *Loaf-Guard* or *Bread Giver*—that is, one who is generous, sustaining, nourishing, protecting, rather than one who dominates. "We do live as human beings with freedom. But everything is dependent on God's sustenance, not just the provision of the 'things we need,' but the source of all our energy, our very life."

Turning to al-Tawba (9):94 and 105—both of which remind humanity that "you will be returned to the Knower of the unseen and the visible, and He will inform you of what you used to do"—a Christian expressed appreciation of the way in which, in these verses, action is combined with belief in God without giving priority to either. "It feels very different from the Christian faith-versus-works debate," he said. But his Muslim colleagues noted the variety of forms of the debate in Islamic tradition. One urged his group to consider especially those strands of the tradition that *discourage* speculative curiosity and metaphysics and emphasize "works only." Others noted that the Qurʾān itself criticizes unnecessary hairsplitting, *not* speculation or metaphysics themselves, and constantly calls people to *reflect*. And one noted that these verses deal with performance before a community. "Think about who you want to please: the righteous or the unrighteous, believers or unbelievers—or God," he suggested. "The theme here is one of sincerity and truthfulness—external visible actions matching internal invisible reality: God sees and judges both." Another offered a Shīʿa perspective, explaining that the Imams and Prophets receive sight and knowledge by their association with God. "That is, they participate in God's knowledge and ability to 'see' the visible and invisible. This shows that foresight and foreknowledge are *not* to be equated with 'determining.' There is no suggestion that the prophets share in 'determining'!"

Calling attention to al-Muddaththir (74):32–47—which includes the assertion, "Every soul is hostage to what it has earned, except the people of the right hand"—a Muslim noted that this passage "echoes the debate regarding the relationship between our actions—in communities—of not praying, not being just and not telling the truth. Again, prayer, action, and truth belong together. We are confronted by the ambiguity of *doing* these things but also of being *led* down a path. The story is about God and human beings but also sinfulness as part of the drama!" Nodding, another Muslim pointed to Āl ʿImrān (3):103, which reads: "Hold fast to God's rope all together; do not split into factions. Remember God's favor to you: you were enemies and then He brought your hearts together and you became brothers by His grace; you were about to fall into a pit of Fire and He saved you from it—in this way God makes His revelations clear to you so that you may be rightly guided." A Christian saw ambiguity in that verse, saying that it seems as though God provides rope for a rescue, but we human beings have to safeguard ourselves by clinging to it—and by doing so *together*.

In another conversation about al-Muddaththir (74):32–47 and notions of free will, one Muslim explained that "the Ashʿarite position is that at any moment in time we acquire the ability to choose an action. It's about what God allots for us." Referring to al-Takwīr (81):29 ("But you will only wish to do so by the will of God, the Lord of all people"), a second Muslim clarified that "the human's ability to will is *within* God's will, it does not delimit God's will. God *gives* you the power to do something, and you acquire it." Be that as it may, one Muslim stressed the importance of God's mercy in the Ashʿarite tradition. Another Muslim cited several in support of the assertion that, with God, justice and mercy always go together; and nothing happens without God's will.

Consideration of the interrelationship between divine justice, mercy, and will, plus the relationship between human moral responsibility and divine sovereignty took place for at least one group in the context of deep comparative discussion of the Joseph Story found in both the Bible and Qur'ān. A Christian explained that, as found in Genesis 50:19–20, it is a wisdom-style narrative, a cause-and-effect story; but at the end there comes a verse that makes it a providential tale about the People of God. As a lesson about human action versus divine sovereignty, said one of the Christians, the biblical Joseph's story is very much a tale of human action but at the end shows us the sovereignty of God. By contrast, a Muslim noted, in the Qur'ānic version, a refrain underscores God's providence. "Human free will and destiny come together. Joseph's life is not being controlled by other people's choices." Calling the Qur'ānic Joseph narrative "a spiritual, universalized version of a Hebrew hero story," one Muslim explained that the classical commentators relied on the Old Testament version to fill in the details. Because the Qur'ān's telling of the Joseph story is explicitly ahistorical and is about possession of special knowledge, he explained, this text has inspired many mystical interpretations. Striking a different tone, a Christian noted that the biblical Joseph text has been used to justify collateral damage in interhuman relations. "Time and again, we are faced with the dilemma of how to relate great harm caused by human beings to divine providence."

Moving on to study of Philippians 2:12–13, a Muslim asked about the meaning of the injunction, "Work out your own salvation." One Christian explained this passage as a reminder that the Christian life is about growing in resonance with God's Word and God's Will. "We are empowered and humbled (struck in awe—in fear and trembling) by the fact that we are called to, need to participate in what God is doing—what is meant by 'salvation.' We have to work it out. But that *is* God at work in us (and this is reassuring—since we are fearful)." Human freedom and God's will and sovereignty must (and do in fact) exist side by side, she stressed. "That's a mystery; but a mystery is *not* a problem to solve. Rather it is something to know, to experience: like love. The more you know it, the greater its mysteriousness becomes."

Conclusion

"When I wrote my paper at the 2015 meeting," said one Christian presenter, "I thought Muslims would disagree with some of my assertions; yet they quoted Muslim sources that say what I said!" At any Building Bridges Seminar, difference is anticipated, even expected. So the degree of commonality found during 2015 discussions was sometimes quite surprising. Upon reflection, many participants felt that distinctions between and within the two traditions were more evident during the seminar's daylong discussion of the subtheme of human action within God's sovereignty (Day Three) than during the days spent on God's creation and its goal (Day One) and the dignity and task of humankind (Day Two). Indeed, one participant asked, "What constitutes (or problematizes) the ground for commonality? Is it our shared academic training and assumptions? Is it our attitude toward texts? Something else?" These questions are worth further consideration when entering into deep dialogue. Whatever the extent of commonality, the success of the Building Bridges Seminar lies in a format that foregrounds serious, exploratory conversation.

Notes

1. This essay is based on notes taken by the author, who sat in on each of the four break-out groups, together with notes taken by one other participant. As has been the case in every annual Building Bridges Seminar report, in this essay the "Chatham House Rule" applies: ideas shared here are unattributed; voices are quoted anonymously; passages in quotations may actually be paraphrases.

2. For Building Bridges Seminar dialogue on the Christian doctrine of the Incarnation, see Michael Ipgrave, ed., *Bearing the Word: Prophecy in Biblical and Qur'anic Perspective* (London: Church House Publishing, 2005). See also, David Marshall, ed., *Communicating the Word: Revelation, Translation, and Interpretation in Christianity and Islam* (Washington, DC: Georgetown University Press, 2011).

ABOUT THE EDITORS

Dr. Lucinda Mosher, assistant academic director of the Building Bridges Seminar, is Faculty Associate in Interfaith Studies at Hartford Seminary.

The Rev. Dr. David Marshall, academic director of the Building Bridges Seminar, is Affiliate Research Fellow of the Berkley Center for Religion, Peace, and World Affairs, Georgetown University, Washington, DC.

CPSIA information can be obtained
at www.ICGtesting.com
Printed in the USA
BVOW08s0727250717
489901BV00002B/5/P